RUNNING TO AMERICA

RUNNING TO AMERICA
AN ATHLETE'S JOURNEY FROM ZIMBABWE

LETIWE MARAKURWA PATTON

MARIGOLD PRESS BOOKS

A division of International School of Story

Copyright © 2024 LETIWE MARAKURWA

All rights reserved. No portion of this book may be reproduced, stored in a retrieval system, or transmitted in any form or by any means–electronic, mechanical, photocopy, recording, scanning, or other–except for brief quotations in critical reviews or articles, without the prior written permission of the author.

Published in Savannah, Georgia by Marigold Press Books, a division of International School of Story.

Marigold Press Books titles may be purchased in bulk for educational, business, fund-raising, or sales promotional use. For information, please email marigoldpressbooks@gmail.com.

Fonts and stock images licensed for commercial use.

Author: Patton, Letiwe Marakurwa
Title: Running to America: An Athlete's Journey from Zimbabwe
ISBN: 9781942923763
Library of Congress Control Number: 2024911929
Cover Design: Bana Balleh, www.banaballeh.com

Printed in the United State of America

For Coach Wayne Phipps

and

In memory of
Coach Michael Chikoto

Table of Contents

Chapter 1 1
Chapter 2 11
Chapter 3 15
Chapter 4 21
Chapter 5 29
Chapter 6 37
Chapter 7 43
Chapter 8 49
Chapter 9 55
Chapter 10 61
Chapter 11 67
Chapter 12 73
Chapter 13 79
Chapter 14 85
Chapter 15 89
Chapter 16 95
Chapter 17 113
Chapter 18 123
Chapter 19 131
Chapter 20 137
Chapter 21 143
Chapter 22 147
Chapter 23 155
Chapter 24 159
Chapter 25 163
Chapter 26 169
Chapter 27 173
Chapter 28 179
Chapter 29 187

Chapter 30	193
Chapter 31	199
Acknowledgements	205
About the Author	207

RUNNING TO AMERICA

Chapter 1

I am the tenth and last child of Onias and Siwisa Marakurwa, Shona-speaking people of the Manyika tribe, and given the name, Letiwe—meaning a gift that comes of God. My birth coincided with the establishment of the Republic of Zimbabwe in 1980, after many years of British colonial rule and civil wars. We lived on land that was our ancestral home. My father was the village chief and my grandfather before him. The line of chiefs in my family goes back as far as anyone can remember. It is an honored and cherished position and not based on wealth. As chief, my father gathered people for meetings and sat in a special chair. He made announcements about the birth of a child, an upcoming marriage ceremony, or a funeral. Sometimes he sent me running to the elders with a message. I felt very important.

As the last-born child, I thought I should be spoiled and pampered. I was wrong. As a girl, I was expected to cook and keep the house cleaned to perfection. The household work fell to my mother and me because my two older sisters, Emma and Tabbeth, were married, and another sister, Jenipher, was away attending the Catholic Makumbe Mission Boarding School in Buhera. I slept on the floor on a *rupasa* and woke to the sound of roosters crowing. More often I awoke to the sound of my mother saying, "*Letiwe muka, vamwe vapedza kurima iwe wakarara.*" "Letiwe, wake up. Others are done farming while you are still sleeping." I did not want to leave my cozy blanket.

On our farm, we grew maize, and after harvesting we took it to a mill and had it ground into cornmeal. *Sadza* was our main staple. We poured cornmeal into a pot of boiling water and stirred it until it thickened to the right consistency. When it cooled, we scooped it up with our right hands and ate it. Sometimes we also had vegetables from our garden. Sadza kept our bellies happy. If there was a cool breeze, we ate outside under a tree. My brothers and I climbed mutohwe trees to get the wild fruit. We chewed it, swallowed the juice, and spit out the pulp. Our elders told us mutohwe fruit would prevent disease. It must have worked because I do not remember ever being sick.

My brothers had the responsibility of caring for our domestic animals. Every day they herded

Chapter 1

cows and goats to the bush to graze. At times I would relieve them so they could go home and eat. I adored my brothers. I was their princess. They played hopscotch with me and taught me how to play soccer. I became competitive and somewhat of a tomboy. Sometimes they sneaked up behind me and hit me playfully just to see how I would react. In the village, a few girls bullied me because my family was poor, but it was just part of everyday life. My brothers taught me how to fight, but I did not want to fight. They told me I must never show weakness by crying in front of my enemies, but sometimes I cried.

My father had a good heart and gave us unconditional love. However, we were strictly disciplined, especially as children of the chief, and I had my share of whippings. When I was very young and got into trouble, my father would tell me to go find a stick he could use to whip me. I would run away. I tried to outrun him, but he was quite a runner, so I was caught. My father always had something to say every night at dinner—about working with a white boss, funny stories about my older siblings, and recollections of his past. He served in the military for many years because it provided reliable and regular wages. All the officers were white and almost all enlisted men were black. He said he and

Running to America

the other enlisted soldiers were mistreated. He did not go into detail, and I think he did not want us to feel bad about his experience. After serving for many years, he retired from the military in 1971 at the age of forty-two. He then worked as a chef at the nearby phosphate mining town of Dorowa, cooking for a lot of mine workers but not getting paid much, because he was not employed by the mining company. He finally told his boss he was leaving. The boss understood and they stayed in touch for many years.

By the time I was born, my father was digging wells for income and working on our farm. The depth of the well depended on the water table. It was dangerous work. If not done correctly, the walls could collapse. My father was very proud of his skill. He dug a well on our property and we used the water for drinking and watering vegetables. But eventually, the well went dry. Every day I walked to the nearest well, filled my drum with water and carried it home balanced on my head. When I was sent to the market on an errand, I was happy because I was out of the house for a while, but my father became angry if I was not home by a certain time, and accepted no excuses, even when I had to wait in long lines. I ran from place to place trying to carry out my tasks on time. It was good

Chapter 1

training for a career in track, although I did not know it at the time.

On my first day of school, I walked with my brothers to Hande Primary School. I was nervous but very excited and could not wait to see what it was like. "Hey Letiwe, if you make a mistake, you will be whipped," taunted a boy. It was not true. Some of my teachers were relatives and I was eager to learn. At lunch, sadza was provided for those of us in grades one through three. We lined up with bowls brought from home. Once we entered fourth grade, we were expected to bring our own food or buy lunch from local vendors. That meant I did not eat lunch. Breakfast for me was tea and bread. A meal of sadza came at the end of the day. It was hard to concentrate when my stomach was empty. Most of my classmates came from wealthier families than mine. The children changed uniforms daily. I only had one school dress and it had a lot of patches. When it got dirty, I washed and pressed it with a coal-heated iron, so it would dry and be ready to wear the next day. I studied at school during the lunch hour because we did not have electricity at home. When the sun went down, we lit candles or used a paraffin-operated light. Candles did not last long but the paraffin would last a few months. We usually went to sleep early because we woke at dawn to work on the farm before school. After the crop-harvesting season we could sleep later.

Although my parents wanted us to get a good education, there were times we could not afford the school fees for tuition, books, and school supplies. Each year a deadline was set for payment. After a few weeks, the headmaster or mistress read aloud the names of the students who were to be sent home for failure to pay. Sadly, my name was frequently on the list. It was heartbreaking. Although I was not the only student in the class required to leave, this indignity only made me stronger and determined to return to school as often as I could. To earn money I worked on a neighbor's farm. The work was in addition to my responsibilities at home and on our farm. Occasionally my father borrowed money so my brothers and I could return to school. As my older brothers obtained jobs, they often helped pay for my education for which I am grateful. I am not sure I ever thanked them. Some of the village children were never given an opportunity to get an education. I was fortunate.

The schools in Zimbabwe were modeled on the British education system and conducted in English. However, our pronunciation was very different from English spoken by the British or Americans. When an American teacher came on

Chapter 1

an exchange program, we did not understand her. It took a while to get used to her pronunciation. All our textbooks were printed in English except for one book printed in Shona about the origin and history of our native languages—Shona and Ndebele. Since I could not afford to buy books, I borrowed and shared textbooks with other students. I read as much as I could and took notes. Often though, I failed to remember what I had read. It was frustrating, but sharing was better than not having a book at all. At home and in our village, we spoke Shona, but our teachers spoke Shona only when necessary to explain something confusing or to help us further understand the subject. My father learned to speak English when he was in the military. I wish my mother could have learned to speak a few words in English. She wanted to talk to my American teacher but held back. The teacher only knew a few words of Shona and my mother knew no English.

When my parents married, my mother was sixteen. My father was a few years older. I admired my mother's strength and courage. She worked harder than any woman I have ever known. She made sure we were all doing well despite the economic challenges we faced. She brought in a little money by crocheting blankets, sweaters, and baby

Running to America

clothes. Sometimes she worked all day for another family in the village, then she came home, worked on our farm, and prepared dinner for us. The extra money she earned never seemed to be enough. At times I saw her crying, but she tried to hide it. She was a private person. When I asked why she was unhappy, she never answered. She always put family first and never complained or argued with my father, who controlled every part of our lives.

In my African Heritage and History class, I learned that Zimbabwe is a Shona word for "stone house" and refers to Great Zimbabwe, once the capital of the kingdom. On a school field trip, I saw this ancient place located in the south-eastern hills of the country. The city was built by placing carved stones on top of each other, rising to an amazing height. The dwellings served many families. When the ruins of Great Zimbabwe were excavated in the late nineteenth century, soapstone carvings of a native bird were unearthed. The Zimbabwe Bird became our national emblem and is prominently portrayed on our national flag.

In the colonial era (1888-1980) the British came, establishing the British South Africa Company to mine the land for a variety of minerals. In 1923 the country was named Southern Rhodesia after Cecil Rhodes, a colonialist mining magnate.

Chapter 1

English became the national language. The Dorowa Mine near my village was mined for phosphate and used for fertilizer. The British took much of the land to mine, and they built cities. However, the British never took our village land. Perhaps it was not suited for their purposes. In 1965 Rhodesia issued a unilateral declaration of independence from Britain. From 1965 through December 1979, a long and bloody civil war pitted two Zimbabwean political and national parties against each other and Britain. I learned about this struggle for power in my history classes. The civil war was never fought in our village, but my parents said local comrades would come by our house asking if their enemies had been seen in the area. They took food from the villagers. Everyone was in fear of being killed. In 1980 the Republic of Zimbabwe was established, followed by more civil unrest. My mother hid when the militants came to our village. They were going house to house telling people they must vote Robert Mugabe for President or be brutalized. During that time jobs were scarce. Many had no way to earn a living.

My father discouraged my brothers from joining the military. However, two of my brothers followed in my father's footsteps. My brother Darlington joined the army in 1986 and worked as a mechanical engineer for almost thirty years. During his service, he was deployed to fight wars in Mozambique and the Congo. My brother Saul joined the military in 1988. He was an army sergeant and an instructor for a parachute regiment.

Chapter 2

My father was a leader at our Methodist church. Men sat on benches on one side of the sanctuary and women sat on the other side of the aisle on floor mats with the children and babies. Sunday School was held after the service and divided into classes based on age. My Sunday School class met inside the church or outside under the trees. I was baptized when I was in primary school. I remember my face was sprinkled with water by the pastor, the *mufundisi*. During the baptism service, the mufundisi read a few Bible verses and the church members sang. After a prayer, he put his hands on my head and blessed me. Our Bible was written in Shona and my father randomly picked verses to read to us. When one of us was ill, he referred to the Bible for a healing verse and followed it with a prayer. I read the Bible occasionally, but it was usually my father who read it to us. He knew his Bible. Before dinner, we always said a prayer.

Each year as the Christmas season approached, I looked forward to the church programs. The Christmas church service was always crowded. One of my sisters was a drummer and I was very proud of her. Drummers were an important part of the music, and they practiced for long hours. They wore special, colorful clothing. We sang to the beats of the drums and swayed in rhythm to the music. The loud joyous sounds filled the air.

One year the church members decided the young people should perform the biblical nativity story about the birth of Jesus. We did not want to have to learn lines and perform in front of the adults. None of the girls wanted to play Mary because, in the Bible story, she was pregnant and unmarried. I got stuck with the role and was very unhappy about it. Fortunately, someone else recited the scripture verses and I just acted out the scene. It was soon over to my great relief, and we continued singing, praying, and enjoying the service. At Christmas, it was customary to decorate the walls of the family gathering room with geometric art. Women came to our house bringing black, red, and white clay-like soil. They applied it to our

Chapter 2

walls and created traditional African artwork. It was bright and cheerful.

For our Christmas meal, my father killed a goat or a cow, depending on how many family members came. The meat was boiled and roasted over an open fire. My mother and I cooked bread, scones, and cake. We could not afford jam, one of the more expensive items. My brothers and sisters came with their families. The house and yard filled with people, laughing and talking. There was no Christmas tree or gift-giving. Christmas was celebrated by going to church, gathering with family, and eating a big meal.

I loved the music at our church, and I knew all the songs by heart. When I was thirteen years old, I attended a church-sponsored youth gathering at a conference center. The main building where we gathered was an open-air structure with an enormous roof. We brought sleeping mats, blankets, pots, and food to cook. The girls slept around a fire and the boys did the same at their campsite. I was elected choir leader for our youth choir. No one else wanted the job. We participated in a competition and our youth choir won. I remember the weekend vividly because I was away from home and enjoying myself.

Every year, school music teachers received a new musical score with lyrics. School choirs rehearsed the score and sang in choir competitions. Even then, I loved competitions. One year we won at the district level and competed in Mutare at the provincial level. My favorite radio singer was Oliver Mtukudzi, popular in South Africa and Zimbabwe. Mukudzi's song, *Shanda*, was my favorite song. Shanda means "work." My mother would say, *Letiwe, shanda nesimba!* "Letiwe, work hard." Though Mtukudzi has passed on, I still listen to his music, and when I do, I get homesick. As a teenager, sometimes I was very angry at God because he allowed us to be poor. I questioned my faith, my life—everything, because I felt hopeless. Neither one of my parents ever seemed to waiver in their faith.

Chapter 3

When I completed the seventh grade, I took the Zimbabwe National Exam and passed. I enrolled in Hande Secondary School, equivalent to high school in America, with Form One through Form Four. I resolved to stay in school hoping it would lead to a good-paying job. My favorite physical education class was track and field, held January through April. Teachers became coaches. We cleared off a field near the school and constructed a dirt track. The area became our sports ground. Distances for races were measured and marked with white chalk. I participated in many events including sprints, middle and long-distance runs, the long jump, high jump, and shot put. We were divided into teams, assigned a team color and a name. Each team tried to earn as many points as possible. I was often on the winning team. We walked many miles to compete against other schools in our district.

When I was fourteen and in Form Two, I discovered I had a talent for running. I competed in all the

Running to America

races from the 100m (0.6 mile) to the 5000m (3.1 mile) race and never got tired. I usually won. For the first time in my life, I was good at something and better at it than the other girls in my school. I knew I had a talent for running but I was not sure what to do with it. I decided to explore my potential and joined the Dorowa Running Club. Dorowa was a small town near the Dorowa Mines and located about six miles from my home. The mines provided good jobs as did the supporting businesses. Over half of the Dorowa Mineworkers lived with their families in nearby villages like ours.

The club was a private athletic organization begun by Michael Chikoto, an accountant at Dorowa Minerals Company. We called him "Coach Chikoto." He had a desire to help young people and influenced my early life tremendously. Athletes who wanted to train at the club were welcomed and it did not cost anything. We met with Coach Chikoto under a tree on the grounds of the mineral company. Sometimes he ran with us. Often the training runs at the club were not over until late in the day. That meant I had to run six miles home alone. I hoped nothing would harm me. It was often pitch-black, and I relied on the headlights of cars and buses to provide light along roadways. I knew there could be wild animals or bad guys out

Chapter 3

there. I always said a prayer asking God to watch over me as I ran.

At the time I joined the running club, my father was in his sixties and manual labor was a bit hard for him. He was still digging wells and farming. He did not know I was going to the Dorowa Running Club. I was too scared to tell him because he was very traditional and thought my place as a girl was in the home. I made sure to get water from the well early in the morning before school. My brothers helped me using big buckets. Even with their help I usually had to go to the well twice to fulfill the needs of my family. If I was home and ready for training, I waited for my father to go to work. When he left the house, I ran to the training club to meet the coach and the other young people. After training I sneaked back in the house and changed out of my workout clothes. If my father asked me where I had been, I lied and made up something.

One night my father caught me sneaking into the house at night. I was wearing running shorts, clothing he did not think a girl should wear in public. He got very angry and yelled at me. It was so loud that our neighbors heard him. I was afraid and embarrassed. I was too scared to tell him I wanted to be an athlete. How would it contribute to my future? My father set the rules in my family.

Shortly after, when my older brother Israel joined the running club, I was also allowed to join because Israel could accompany me. It was not fair, but I held my tongue. When Israel dropped out of the club to study for his Form Four exams, I continued training at the club and sneaked into the house before my father knew I had been gone. Most of the girls in my school did not have issues with their fathers and hung out with friends at night. Their fathers were more lenient.

    The tension with my father eased a bit when Coach Chikoto came to our house to ask my father to allow me to join the running club. He let my parents know I would be in good hands. Gradually my father allowed me to train and enter track competitions. Coach handled the paperwork and organized transportation. I excelled in cross-country races, and I was allowed to do the cross-country workout with the boys because they were more challenging. We avoided running too close to the phosphate mines because the air was polluted. We ran on trails, over bridges, up and around hills. The scenery was beautiful. I ran in all types of weather. Coach said, "If weather affects your running, then you are not ready to train." Once I ran a 5km (3.10 mile) cross-country course over hilly terrain on a

Chapter 3

foggy, cold day. I was energized and easily won the race.

Coach entered me in racing events sponsored by private businesses and clubs. These races were sponsored by organizations such as the Zimbabwe Republic Police, the Zimbabwe Dairy Board, and the Coca-Cola Company. Prizes were given to winners, and I won school supplies, notebooks, pencils, and rulers—items I was not able to afford otherwise. I also won bowls, plates, cups, and other household items. It was such a joy for me to bring home my prizes. A local newspaper published the names of the winners of the events and a few people in my neighborhood stopped to talk with me. Even my father seemed pleased.

Chapter 4

The offices of the Dorowa Minerals Company were located on secured and gated property. Coach Chikoto had access to the buildings. On days when we were to compete in Mutare, about 62 miles away, we spent the night in the lobby of the Dorowa Minerals administration building. It was not the most comfortable place to sleep, but it had electricity, clean running water, and benches. Coach was also able to get a company bus. We woke up very early in the morning and got on the road. We never stayed in a hotel because we could not afford it. Coach had a big heart and was not paid to train us. Often, he used his own money to buy us food when we were traveling. Sometimes we carried cooking pots and cornmeal and stopped in the middle of nowhere to make a fire and cook sadza.

When I ran cross-country, the natural terrain was easier on my feet than running on a hard surface. Since we did not have running shoes and could not afford them, Coach purchased track shoes and distributed them for use at practice and races. After the race, he collected the shoes to store in his office. I never wore running shoes, preferring to run barefoot, but Coach asked me to try them. He thought they might help me run faster. I tried on a pair, but they were uncomfortable and added weight to my feet, slowing me down. There was no requirement to wear track shoes, so I decided not to wear them. When I continued to win races, I was certain I did not need shoes. However, sometimes I developed blisters. The blisters did not slow me down but treating them was a challenge. My father said ointment would make it worse and we could not afford band-aids. He told me to put water in a bucket and leave it outside at night. It was winter and icy cold. The next morning, as instructed by my father, I stood with my feet in a bucket of freezing water for as long as I could tolerate it. After a few days of this routine, the blisters gradually went away.

Both of my parents were fast runners when they were young. They each bragged that I had inherited their running genes. My mother said, *Ndaimhanya sitereki setsuro uye hapana aindibata*, "I used to run fast like a rabbit, and nobody could catch me." My father, on the other hand, would casually say, *Letiwe mwanangu, inini ndini ndakakupa chipo*

Chapter 4

chekumhanya nekuti ndaisiya vanhu vese pandaive muchisoja, "Letiwe, my daughter, I am the one who gave you the running talent because I used to be the fastest runner in the army."

As a teenager, my thoughts turned to boys. At school, I began to notice boys talking to girls they liked. The boys initiated the conversations. If a boy did not take an interest in you, then you were out of luck. It was a huge deal to have a boyfriend and there were a lot of couples in my class. I had my eye on a few boys and hoped one of them would speak to me, but I was shy and a loner. Then I noticed one boy eyeing me a lot and he was good-looking. What was I going to do? Should I encourage him? Under Coach Chikoto's guidance, our team operated with strict discipline. Every Friday we had a meeting called "The Round Table." We talked about team goals, upcoming meets, and other items on the agenda. One Friday coach led a discussion about boy-girl relationships. Coach told us not to date and to focus on running and school. He knew we were not ready to have serious relationships, and he was right. A few girls got pregnant and had to either drop out of school to get married or ended up being single mothers at a young age. Despite this warning from Coach Chikoto, some of my teammates dated secretly, thinking he would not find out. When Coach did learn about it, he banned them from practice and from traveling to track meets. A few teenagers left on their own because running track was not as important to them as dating and forming relationships. The opposite was true for me. I wanted more than anything to become a track athlete and I did not want to do anything that would jeopardize that goal. If it meant I had to postpone dating, then so be it.

Coach Chikoto often said, "I am both your father and mother, and if anything goes wrong, I will be held responsible." He was like a second father, but more importantly, he was my mentor. He told me he was proud of me. No one had ever said that to me. Coach invested considerable time and effort into refining my training program. He recognized my potential and pushed me relentlessly to maximize it. His training sessions were grueling. My parents gradually accepted my passion for running track. They let me catch up on my chores over the weekends. However, when the land needed plowing or harvesting, I missed workouts. We had to put food on the table. Coach frequently asked us how we were doing in school. I said that I was doing ok, but in truth, I was struggling. I was exhausted from the demands of school, training, traveling, and working on the farm. Luckily, the

Chapter 4

headmistress was flexible. I took an exam earlier than everyone else because I was scheduled to travel to a track meet on the day of the test. At the end of Form Two, I sat for the Zimbabwe Junior Certificate examinations. To my great relief, I passed and advanced to Form Three.

After winning school-sponsored races in my district, I was eligible to compete in my province, one of ten in the country. I won the Manicaland Province Cross-Country Race in Mutare and was selected to represent my province at the national level in the capital city of Harare. Harare was magical—lights, cars, tall buildings, parks with flowers and trees, and people everywhere. I was excited but somewhat scared because I heard stories about outsiders getting lost and robbed. I did not plan to go anywhere by myself. The race took place in the Harare National Sports Stadium. I had never raced on a real track. It felt good to walk barefoot on the manicured grounds. I saw girls from other provinces warming up and doing practice runs. I tried not to be distracted. I decided it was a "do or die" race for me. I would discover if I really had competitive running skills. If I lost, well, I did not want to think about losing. I said a short prayer, "Lord, help me to do my best. You have shown me the talent that I have, so let me shine." When

Running to America

the gun went off, I raced my guts out. I remember the bright lights illuminating the track and the cheering crowd. When I was awarded the medal for first place, I had tears of joy. At fifteen, I was the Junior Women's Cross Country Champion of Zimbabwe. My climb to the top happened over the course of one year. It was surreal.

What I discovered next was even more exciting. Athletes who competed and won on the national level received monetary prizes. Coach entered me into corporate-sponsored track events in Harare. With each race, my goal was to place in the top three so I would be awarded a monetary prize. One time I took home a significant amount of prize money. It was like winning a million dollars because I knew how far it would go. I dutifully gave it to my father. He called my mother and brothers and we gathered at the table where he counted the money. He gave it all to my mother to buy food and whatever she needed in the house. He told her to be sure she paid the school fees and any debts we owed to neighbors. He was in full control of the money, as are most men in my culture. He did not give me any portion of it, nor did I ask for any. But winning was a big deal to me and I did not feel appreciated. Nonetheless, I knew they were proud of me. When we were alone, my mother thanked

Chapter 4

me for winning money for the family and said she would pray for the Lord to continue to give me energy, speed, and the will to keep running. She did not feel comfortable saying much around my father. I wish my parents could have seen me run in a competition, but they never did.

Chapter 5

After winning at the national level I became eligible to compete for Zimbabwe on an international level. The International Women's Junior Cross Country Division was a category for girls under the age of twenty. The Zimbabwe National Athletic Association was a federation of qualified coaches, officials, and administrators who oversaw athletic competitions throughout the country. They made final selections as to who would be selected to compete in the international events. I was certain I would not be selected, because it cost a lot of money to travel overseas. My mother said it was about the performance and not money. She was right. When I heard my name announced by an official, it was unbelievable. I was going to the international world cross-country championships! Everyone said they were proud of me. I was proud of myself. I began to believe that anything was possible.

Athletes were required to attend a training camp in Harare for two weeks. Coach Chikoto spoke to my father, who agreed I could go with the team. Coach told him the Zimbabwe National Athletics Association would take care of all the expenses including pocket money. Coach drove us to Harare where we met the coaches, officials, and other track athletes who would be representing Zimbabwe. Most of the athletes spoke Shona but with differing dialects representing sub-groups of the Shona tribes. A few spoke Ndebele. I met Chipo Dzikiti from Mutare who was also in the junior women's category. A member of the association helped me with my application. When I was handed my passport, my upcoming journey became real. My parents were understandably concerned about their fifteen-year-old daughter traveling to another part of the world. It was a lot for them to process. It was a lot for *me* to process. In the end, they trusted Coach Chikoto to look after my interests. Simply put, without Coach, I would never have had the opportunities that came my way. He encouraged me to continue working hard and to always remember where I came from. He emphasized the importance of staying grounded. "Don't forget the people who played a role in your journey," he said, "including

Chapter 5

parents, peers and teachers. Stay connected to them throughout your journey."

The Zimbabwe Broadcasting Corporation filmed an interview with me, but when it aired I missed it. I was training at the running club. We did not have a television, so it did not matter. A few of my neighbors told me they saw the interview. During an assembly at school, the headmistress called me to come down to the front of the room and I was acknowledged for my accomplishments. My classmates joked that I was a star in the making, coming out of nowhere. I felt privileged to represent my beautiful nation and to compete against other talented athletes from countries all over the world.

In Harare, I met Joseph Mungwari, our team official, and Robert Mutsauki, the President of the Zimbabwe National Athletic Association. Our team was made up of seven males and three females. I was the youngest. We went on cross-country training runs and were given details about travel and accommodations. Uniforms were issued. We were required to take good care of our uniforms because we were to return them after the competition. The young women wore off-white skirts and green blazers with the national emblem, the Zimbabwe Bird. The uniforms also had emblems with the colors of the national flag. I was proud of my uniform. Mr. Mutsauki was very supportive of the team and certain we would not disappoint the fans back home. We later learned we were going to Budapest, Hungary. I had no idea where Hungary was, and it did not occur to me to look at a map to see where my journey would take me.

As far as I knew, I was the first student to represent Hande Secondary School at national and international cross-country events. At the time, the best world track athletes, particularly distance runners, were from East African countries like Ethiopia and Kenya. My role model was Julia Sakala, one of the best mid-distance runners in Zimbabwe. She won medals at numerous international competitions and her picture was on TV and billboards. When I learned she would be on the Zimbabwe team I was thrilled. I was very shy though and did not speak to her. I was not sure what I would say. She was about nine years older than me and famous. When we did finally talk, she was very friendly. I told her I had always looked up to her. In my culture, respect for an older person is shown by calling them "brother, sister, aunt, uncle" and so forth. I asked Julia if I could call her "sister" and

Chapter 5

she said I could. She inspired me to push myself harder. I wanted to be like her.

In March 1994 I received my airline ticket. As I boarded the airplane, I was nervous and had crazy butterflies in my stomach. The takeoff was noisy until the plane leveled off. I realized flying was not so bad. The seats and windows were small. I thought I would be able to look down and see all the houses below and was disappointed when I only saw clouds and then darkness. The flight attendant handed out snacks. I quickly ate mine, but it certainly did not fill me up. I asked the attendant for more.

Budapest was cold. I was glad I had a warm uniform and traveling shoes. A shuttle bus took us to a hotel where many of the athletes were staying. It was like an athlete village. Chipo Dzikiti and I were roommates. Our meals in the dining hall were buffet-style, and we could choose whatever we wanted to eat. I had never seen so much food! It was overwhelming. The athletes sat at tables with their teams. I did not want to look out of place and glanced over to other tables to see what utensils were used. The food looked interesting, and I found most of it to be delicious. Communication was hard because of the language barrier but I smiled and waved at everyone. I found a few athletes who spoke English and were able to converse a little.

Like the International Olympics, the athletes from each country participated in an opening ceremony and parade. The race was to be held at the Kincsem Park in Budapest on a beautifully manicured racecourse used for horse racing. During the days before the race we were allowed to run at Kincsem Park so we could become familiar with the course. I was entered in the 4.3 km (2.6 miles) race in the Junior Women's Division and was up against experienced runners. Suddenly, I felt exhausted. I was not used to the time changes, but I kept training. I did not want to let my country down and was determined to perform well. On the day of the race, the weather was cold and windy. As we lined up, I noticed I was not the only athlete to run barefoot. The ground was cold and sprinkled with snow. When the gun went off, I ran as fast as I could. I was aware of cheering from Zimbabwe fans in the stands. I gave it everything I had. When I finished, my feet were numb. Officials handed out tin foil wraps for warmth. Teammates came and stood on either side helping to support me. I hobbled to our tent and anxiously waited for the results. Out of 142 participants from 39 countries, I finished 22nd overall. An error in the statistics switched my name

Chapter 5

in the records with Chipo Dzikiti, who placed 29th. The top three winners, as I predicted, were from Kenya. In Zimbabwe, only the top three winners are considered as having importance, so I did not see myself as a winner. Either you placed in the top three or you didn't place at all.

One day before the trip ended, our bus driver took us to a nice downtown area so we could walk around. Budapest was a beautiful city. We were given pocket money to spend on souvenirs. It was not much, but I knew my family was struggling and I could not spend it. The money would go a long way toward paying for my school fees. I walked around and looked at everything. When teammates asked why I was not buying anything, I told them that I did not see anything that interested me. They did not know about my personal struggles, and I did not want to talk about them. Back home, I proudly paid for my own school fees. I passed the exams and completed Form 3. I had one more year of school to go.

Chapter 6

A few months later, I was selected by the Zimbabwe National Athletics Association to travel with my team manager, Stanley Madhiri, to Lisbon, Portugal, where I competed in the 3000m (1.86 mile) race for the World Junior Track and Field Championships for women under twenty years of age. I was the only athlete from Zimbabwe, and the Association paid the expenses. The stadium was packed. The race was broadcast on TV, and I finished in 8th place overall. I do not remember much except traveling to and from the event. My goal was to get to the track, perform well, and travel back home.

I then represented Zimbabwe at the Engen Grand Prix in Cape Town, South Africa. The Grand Prix was an annual, global circuit of one-day outdoor track and field competitions. The top athletes were invited to compete by the International Association of Athletic Federations. I had accumulated enough points in track meets to be eligible. The athletes were fast, and I followed their pace, seeing it as an opportunity to improve my time. I enjoyed racing even though I did not win any money. Next, I entered and won the 5000m (3.1 mile) race at the Southern Regional Championships, represented by fifteen countries from all over Southern Africa. I was on home soil, and it was a great experience.

As my athletic competition opportunities grew, my school attendance went down. Sometimes I was away for two weeks at a time. My schedule was exhausting. I was in my second year of international competition and already overwhelmed. In 1995 I qualified again for the Junior Women's World Cross-Country Championships in Durham, England. The race was held in March at the University of Durham and the distance was 4.47km, about 2.8 miles. I was the top Zimbabwean athlete competing in the race. Out of 109 junior women athletes from 33 countries, I placed 24th. A young woman from Finland won and in 2nd and 3rd place were the Kenyans.

In April, I broke two long-standing records in junior track competition: one on April 3rd in St. Petersburg, South Africa in the 3000m race with a time of 9:45 and the other a few weeks later on

Chapter 6

April 29th in Harare—the 5000m with a time of 17:08:85.

After the spring races, I took some time off to prepare for the All-Africa Games. I was selected to compete as part of the Zimbabwe National Team based on my performance in international races. The All-Africa Games were hosted by Zimbabwe in September 1995. Thankfully the games were held in Zimbabwe's capital, Harare, so I didn't have to travel a long distance. I went to the training camp and missed three weeks of school. However, I loved the opportunity to live in the athlete's village and make friends with athletes from other parts of Africa. I ran the 5000m but did not do well. I had hoped that being on home turf, my speed would improve. But the Kenyans and Ethiopians won again. It was frustrating, but I was tough mentally. I ran my best before the home crowd and improved my time in that event.

At the end of my Form 4 school year I took the O Level National exams with my classmates. There were five separate tests, each one a different subject. Once the tests were over, we waited months before getting scores from the Ministry of Education. Grades were not released unless fees were paid. When the test scores came out in March 1996, I was in Stellenbosch, Western Cape, South Africa participating in the 4.22km Junior Women's World Cross Country Championships, held at the Danie Craven Stadium. It was my third time competing at the world cross-country race. I was surprised at how cold it was in South Africa. Once again snow was scattered in places on the track. With 115 athletes from 30 nations participating, I came in 43rd. I was the top runner representing Zimbabwe and becoming one of the promising young distance runners in the country. Expectations for me to excel were high.

In July 1995, I represented Zimbabwe at the Under-20 African Junior Athletic Championships in the Ivory Coast. It was my first trip to West Africa. In Abidjan, I was shocked to see a few locals washing themselves outside on the streets. They used water jugs and cups and poured water on their feet, legs, and heads. The people were dressed in traditional, colorful African clothing. The local food was spicy and delicious. I ate fish and plantains, both new to me. I enjoyed being in an African culture different from my own. At the track meet, I competed in the women's 1500m, placing 5th, and the 3000m, placing 4th. I was one place short of a medal. It was frustrating.

When I arrived home, I reviewed my school test scores. I did not do well. I only passed three

Chapter 6

of the five tests. I signed up to take three courses and planned to sit for the tests in November 1996. If I passed two of the tests, I could complete Form 4. There was no graduation ceremony. Either you passed or did not. I had no plans for my future once I completed secondary school. I was not headed to university.

At the peak of my training, tragedy struck. My brother, Saul, who was in the military, passed away after an illness leaving a wife and seven-year-old son. We gathered at home to grieve. In my village, the notice of a death comes when women make shrill high-pitched sounds that alert others. The wailing passes from woman to woman until the whole village knows there has been a death. Saul's coffin was placed in our home where family and mourners gathered for three days before the burial. He received a military funeral and was buried in the family cemetery behind our house. Soldiers provided the coffin and dug his grave. A military uniform, medals, and a Zimbabwean flag were placed in the casket. When the time came to bury him, the military guard carried his coffin to the cemetery. As part of the ritual, they marched a few steps at a time, laid the coffin on the ground, said a few words about Saul, sang a few songs, and continued in this manner until they reached his

Running to America

resting place. The sergeant gave a speech about Saul serving his country. They fired shots in the air and saluted. It was moving, and I think everyone felt Saul had been a great military serviceman. I was heartbroken. I missed my big brother.

In the summer of 1996, I turned eighteen. It was time to stop training, traveling, and competing and do something else. But working on the farm was all I could see for myself. My future looked bleak. I took additional classes and exams and finally passed Form 4. I had no idea my life was about to change forever.

Chapter 7

The 1996 Olympic Summer Games were held in America. In 1990, Atlanta, Georgia was selected as the site for the games. Georgians were ecstatic. The mayor of the City of LaGrange, Georgia was eager for the city to become involved. LaGrange was a former cotton mill town where Africans once were slaves. The citizens wanted to change their image and demonstrate that bringing people together from diverse backgrounds could foster understanding and broaden perspectives. LaGrange was selected as one of four international track and field training hubs for Olympic Solidarity, a program of the International Olympic Committee designed to assist athletes from developing countries.

In the years leading up to the 1996 Olympics, the LaGrange community hosted players from all over the world. The athletes lived in dorms at LaGrange College, ate in the cafeteria, attended local schools and colleges, and trained at facilities provided by the city. As a result, fifteen athletes

Running to America

who trained in LaGrange competed in the games held in Atlanta. When the 1996 games ended, the Olympic Committee began planning for the 2000 Summer Olympic Games to be held in Sydney, Australia. The City of LaGrange planned to continue hosting the training center for athletes through Olympic Solidarity.

Zimbabwe qualified as a country eligible for Olympic Solidarity Scholarships. In 1997, the Zimbabwe National Athletic Association applied through Olympic Solidarity for scholarships for Zimbabwean athletes to train for the 2000 Summer Olympic Games. Zimbabwe was awarded three scholarships. One day I was training at the Dorowa Running Club when Coach Chikoto called me into his office. The President of the Zimbabwe National Athletic Association had contacted him by phone. Coach told me I was one of three Zimbabwean track and field athletes selected to receive a scholarship through Olympic Solidarity to train for the Sydney, Australia 2000 Summer Olympic Games. I was to move to America and train in LaGrange, Georgia.

I could not believe it! I was going to train to compete in the Olympics. It was a dream come true. I ran home and told my parents. Neither one showed much reaction. I knew they were trying to absorb this shocking news. I was also trying

Chapter 7

to absorb it. The other two athletes selected were George Maringapasi, a high jumper, and Norma Jean Harry, a sprinter. I was to train as a distance runner. All three of us were about eighteen years of age.

During this significant and emotional time, I realized God had not given up on me and I was grateful. I spent the weekend fasting and praying to demonstrate my thankfulness to God, for keeping me strong through all my struggles and for giving me this great opportunity. At times I teared up. I wondered if I was dreaming. Never could I have imagined leaving everyone I knew to live in the United States, where I knew no one. A voice inside me said, "Take this opportunity." I had faced hardships all my life. I could do this. Coach Chikoto phoned my headmistress, Mrs. Mildred Chikuruwo, to share the news with her. She was very happy and told me how proud she was of my accomplishments. She was like a second mother. She knew sometimes I had dropped out of school for failure to pay fees and was always understanding when I missed school due to national and international competitions. Mrs. Chikuruwo and I discussed the procedures required for transferring my school records to an American school.

Not only would I be moving to America, I could also further my education.

When news about my scholarship was made public, I was interviewed and filmed by a Zimbabwean news team. "I am very thankful for the opportunity to be part of the Olympic Solidarity Program," I said. "It is an honor to represent my training club and my country. I want to do my best and not disappoint the people who believe in my potential." Coach Chikoto gave me challenging workouts as I continued my training. After a required physical examination, he drove me to Harare where I met with Mr. Robert Mutsauki, who gave me details about the International Training Center in LaGrange, Georgia. He assured me I had enough time to prepare for my journey.

My father did not quite like the idea of me moving to another country so far away. He probably could have stopped me from going to America and crushed my dream for a better life. He did not. However, it was a long time before he accepted the fact that he was losing a daughter. As the date to leave home came closer, I saw my mother go off by herself and cry. She went about her work singing her favorite hymn, *Hakuna zita Serajesu*, "There is no name like Jesus." It was the hymn she sang when she was sad. She said, "*Handizivi kuti*

Chapter 7

ndichazokuonawo here mwanangu. "I am not sure I will ever see you again, my child." *Zvino zvawave kuenda uchapiwa mari here yekutitumira tigotengawo chikafu mumba*? "Now that you are leaving, will they give you money you can send home so we can buy food?" I desperately hoped I would receive spending money. My financial contribution was essential to the well-being of my parents. My siblings had families of their own to support. My father was acting strong, but my mother knew he was struggling with my departure. My mother became so distraught at one point that my father said, "*Musacheme, ngatinamateyi mwana afambe zvakanaka,*" "Don't cry. Let's pray so our child can travel safely." My parents and a few siblings gathered for a send off prayer with me the night before I left for Harare. The 2000 Olympic Summer Games were three years away. I did not know when I would return home.

Coach Chikoto drove me to Harare. He dropped me off at the office where I was to report. I completed the paperwork and a few days later, I left for the airport. No one in my family could travel to the airport to see me off. As I stood with George and Norma Jean, ready to board, I saw Coach Chikoto walk up. I was so happy to see him. It meant so much to me that he came. He later went to tell my parents that things went well.

Chapter 8

The flight was long and uneventful. We landed at the Hartsfield-Atlanta International Airport at night. I knew it was night, but the airport was lit up like day. One of the coaches and the General Manager of the International Training Center came to meet us and drove us southwest of Atlanta to LaGrange, Georgia. I had no idea where I was geographically. I was tired but excited. We moved into LaGrange College student dormitories where I was paired with Justine Nahimana from Burundi. She spoke only French, so our communication was minimal. Whenever she wanted to say something to me, she asked one of her countrymen to translate to English or she just pointed to things. I think I was paired with her because she was also a distance runner. Somehow, we made it work. I learned that Abdi Bile from Somalia was to be our distance running coach. Bile participated in the 1996 Summer Olympics in Atlanta. He ran the 1500m for Somalia and finished 6th in the men's final. He was offered and accepted a position as a coach at the International Training Center. I was excited to have a world-class track coach. Later Diodone Kwizera from Burundi was also named as a coach. We were in good hands.

The first few weeks I did not venture far from the training center. I was afraid of getting lost. The city had a nice track and field facility. I walked to and from the track with other athletes. I greeted almost every person I saw but often did not get a response. I was very lonely and homesick and not sure if I had made the right decision. Sometimes I socialized with teammates but more often I went to my room or walked outside for fresh air. Time zones between Zimbabwe and the eastern United States were very confusing. It took me a while to figure out the difference. I was seven hours behind Zimbabwean time. It was difficult to reach my parents by phone. I worried about them. I was happy and relieved to learn I was to receive a $60.00 monthly stipend. I used Western Union cables to send money home. One of my siblings had access to a bank. The money was collected and taken to my parents. At that time the currency rate of the Zimbabwe dollar to the U.S. dollar was good, so the money went a long way. My parents and I corresponded, but it took close to a month for

Chapter 8

a letter to arrive by mail. I sensed I was the only athlete sending money home. The food prepared for us was a huge problem because it was often fried. Fried food tasted good for a minute, but it was not nourishing. I needed well-balanced meals given the intensity of the workouts. I did not know why athletes were not given healthy food. But we had bigger problems.

In LaGrange, the enthusiasm for sponsoring the International Training Center was fading now that the 1996 Olympic Summer Games were over. The training center was in a financial crisis due to mismanagement by an out-of-state administrator. There was no money left, so the LaGrange Sports Authority decided to close the center. One day an International Olympic Committee representative told us to pack our things. We were moving. Some athletes left the program because they were not asked to be involved in the selection of a new location for the training center. Others left to return home or decided to go to other training centers. The number of track and field athletes decreased to about two dozen. Most were from Africa. I knew nothing about why we were moving. I packed my suitcase and wondered where I was going. I hoped my mail would be forwarded.

On July 23, 1997 we were bused to Savannah, Georgia, a southern coastal city on the Atlantic Ocean. When the LaGrange International Training Center closed, a new training center was urgently needed in Georgia to continue the Olympic Solidarity Program. The Greater Savannah Sports Council came to the rescue and agreed to find a location. The Sports Council had played a key role during the 1996 Olympic Games. The Finn Men's Competition, a sailing event, was held in Savannah from July 22, 1996, to August 2, 1996. Olympic athletes were transported daily to Wassaw Sound, an inland bay that opened to the Atlantic Ocean, where offshore sailing competitions took place. Over 1,000 volunteers provided logistics.

After conferring with the Savannah Sports Council, the International Olympic Committee agreed to allocate funds. The IOC's goal was to send enough athletes to Savannah to fund the program and cover costs for staff, housing, coaches, athletic clothing, and equipment. Unlike the huge publicity Savannah received during the 1996 Summer Olympics, people were largely unaware that a small

Chapter 8

number of athletes had moved to town to train for the 2000 Olympic Summer Games.

Chapter 9

The City of Savannah was beautiful and diverse. The people I met were welcoming. In September the weather was at its best, not too hot and not too cold. But Savannah did not seem prepared to receive us. First, we were placed in the Chatham Nursing Home on LaRoche Avenue in an unoccupied building at the back of the property. It was obvious that nobody had lived there for years. Soon the Savannah Sports Council moved us again, to a vacant building on Skidaway Road just south of Savannah State University, a historically black college. The building was known locally as "Cohen's Old Men's Retreat" and had served as a retirement home for fifty years before closing. The large brick building was located on land with moss-draped oak trees. White columns stood in the center of the building and the one-story structure spread out on either side like wings. It had been uninhabited for many years but was in better shape than the nursing home. The building was designed to house one person in each room. The rooms were not big but each of us had space and privacy. The beds were twin-sized and comfortable. We were each responsible for cleaning our rooms. Bathrooms in the hall were designed for the disabled and elderly. There were not enough showers for everyone to use at the same time, so we took turns. Since I had no experience living in America and nothing to compare it to, I never questioned my circumstances. Women were placed on one wing of the building and men on the other. A curfew was set, and the main door was locked at night. Fortunately, we never had an emergency. I guess we would have jumped out the windows if we needed to. Coaches used part of the building for offices during the day but went home at night. Communication was generally between the administrators and our coaches. Fortunately, our coaches transferred with us from LaGrange to Savannah. Occasionally we had team meetings to discuss the program.

At Savannah Technical College we were tested on our knowledge of English. Most of the athletes were from French-speaking nations. At the training center, we all spoke English out of necessity and took English courses, but at different levels. Athletes who qualified enrolled in Savannah State University, Armstrong College, now Georgia Southern Uni-

Chapter 9

versity Armstrong Campus, or Savannah Technical College. A few obtained scholarships. The younger ones enrolled in private high schools like Savannah Country Day and St. Vincent's Academy. Some athletes decided not to continue their education. It was optional.

My family could not pay tuition for a private school, so Rob Dailey, an administrator, took me to Jenkins High School, a public high school where tuition and fees were not required. I was the only one from my training center program to attend Jenkins. We met with the principal who requested copies of my transcripts from Hande Secondary School in Zimbabwe. I was placed in 11th grade and signed up for courses including American Government and U.S. History, required in Georgia for a high school diploma. I selected French as my language study course. I was nineteen and one of the oldest students, but it didn't bother me. I was given an opportunity to get an education and I was grateful. I received textbooks for free and did not have to share the books with other students as I had at Hande Secondary School. Steven Lugor, one of the athletes, was the team driver. We had a van for transportation and every day Steven made the rounds of the schools we were attending, dropping off and picking us up.

At Jenkins, I had difficulty understanding the accents of the students and they had trouble understanding me, although we were all speaking English. I especially could not understand the accent of the black students. In the cafeteria, as I moved my tray down the line of food displayed, I tried to convey a selection verbally to the lady behind the counter. I did not understand her, nor did she understand me. Thankfully I could just point. I was frequently asked, "Where are you from?" Most of the students had never heard of Zimbabwe and did not know where it was located geographically. "It is the country just above South Africa," I said. Students thought Africa was a country. "No," I said. "Africa is a continent." They shrugged their shoulders and moved on. I wish American students were taught more about African nations. I was not allowed to be on the track team at Jenkins High School. Officials determined that training at the International Training Center disqualified me from competing for a local high school. I did not have time for it anyway.

At the training center, we ate in a dining room inside the building and were given a menu for each day. The food we were served was bland. I did not

Chapter 9

care for the fish patties or greens. The vegetables were not tasty, and I was not sure if they were cooked fresh or from a can. The fried chicken was good but greasy. Some athletes ate a little bit of whatever we were served, then walked down the street to a Chinese restaurant and ordered take-out. I could not afford it. We were not usually allowed to cook anything in the kitchen for liability and safety reasons. On rare occasions though, we were able to cook on weekends. The West Africans made the best dishes. A city official gave us movie passes so we could enjoy seeing films. I went to a movie theater for the first time. When we were taken to the Savannah Mall, I got lost. It was nothing like the market at home. I longed to speak Shona and searched for George, who traveled with me from Zimbabwe. It was comforting to converse in my mother tongue. George made me laugh and it felt good.

Chapter 10

The Olympic Committee provided equipment for us including running shoes and tracksuits. "What is your shoe size?" I was asked. "I don't know," I said. I had no experience buying shoes and never learned my shoe size. I tried on shoes until the coach determined a size suitable for me. I did not want to wear running shoes at all, especially ones with spikes. But I was given no choice. I finally faced the fact that I would have to wear shoes in competitive races. It was terrible. I struggled for months. My toes could not breathe. I could not focus on racing. My feet felt heavy and the shoes slowed me down. They looked nice, but they were my worst enemy. My coaches told me I would eventually get used to them. I did not believe them. Not one bit! But after about three months, to my surprise, I did get used to them. However, just as I became comfortable wearing running shoes, the administration changed shoe sponsors. We were initially issued Reeboks and then Asics. Each design change required adjustment. When I wasn't training, I often jogged barefooted, and it came as no surprise to my teammates, most of whom were from Africa. I knew they had also gone barefooted as children. As shoes wore out, the IOC issued us new ones, so thankfully I did not have to buy my own shoes.

We trained at the Savannah State University Track and Field Complex, which was within walking distance. Our primary training coaches continued to work with us. I did not have a chance to interact with Savannah State University athletes because we used the track facility late in the afternoon after they had gone. A couple of athletes in our program attended SSU and a few even received scholarships.

My favorite place to run in Savannah was at Lake Meyer. The trail went around a lake in a park filled with beautiful trees and green grass. Pathways provided safety so I did not have to run in a street or trespass on anyone's yard. As I began competing in races, I adjusted to new workout schedules and racing priorities. I needed to run a certain speed to qualify for the next level of competition, especially at the collegiate level and beyond. I was told to run hard and do my best. I competed in cross-country events all over the South and against some of the

Chapter 10

best athletes. I had a few disappointments here and there. I set very high expectations for myself. At times I would start the race well but run out of energy before it was over. My scholarship did not have a timeline, but there were expectations of me both on the track and in the classroom.

We were allowed a ten-minute telephone call monthly, paid for by the program. Due to the expense of calling countries outside of the United States, we were timed. We could not go over ten minutes. Phoning home was a stressful experience because my parents had no phone. An administrator started the clock running and I frantically used up two or three minutes calling the market across the street from home. I quickly hung up as I waited for someone to notify my parents. After a while, I called the store again hoping one of my parents picked up. I talked to my mother more than my father because she was usually the one at home. My father was always out and about, but I talked to him a few times. I was grateful for the opportunity to call and check on them, but there was little time to talk in detail. My father rarely talked much and wanted to hear how I was doing. My parents wrote letters. I read them over and over. I kept a box with letters from family and friends but lost it somewhere in all my moving around. I was devastated when I found it gone.

When I first arrived in America, my best friends were my countrymen, George and Norma Jean, primarily because we spoke the same language. Over time I met and made friends with athletes from other countries. We were a diverse group, speaking many languages. English was our common denominator. Ruth Mangue was a sprinter from Equatorial Guinea. It took a while for us to fully warm up to each other because she spoke Spanish and French, and I spoke neither. She called me "Lee" and gradually we became friends. She said I was a tomboy because of the way I dressed, and the fact that I had close-cropped hair. It was customary in Zimbabwe for girls to have close-cropped hair, especially in rural areas. I was very comfortable with it. It was normal and practical, and it cost money to style longer hair. Over time I sported different hairstyles.

I usually wore baggy pants, very loose T-shirts or tops and sneakers. I did have a dress or two but no dress shoes. I never wore jewelry other than my running watch. My father told me that make-up and long nails were for prostitutes. Nevertheless, I tried putting on make-up, but it was not my style. Ruth had a great voice and enjoyed singing. We

Chapter 10

explored churches in the area. Our desire to find a place to worship was something we had in common.

Tina Paulino was from Mozambique, right across the border from Zimbabwe and not far from my home. She spoke a dialect of Manyika. Tina was more of a middle-distance sprinter, but she could compete in any distance run. I knew of her because she came to Zimbabwe in 1995 for the All-Africa Games held in Harare. I did not get to talk to her at the All-Africa Games, but I saw her compete. Tina and her teammate ran the women's 800-meter and came in first and second place. It was a great day for Mozambique. Beginning in 1995, Tina was able to benefit from the Olympic Solidarity Program and trained for the 1996 Olympic Games in LaGrange. A local newspaper reported that Tina turned in an impressive performance in the Atlanta Grand Prix. She followed the program as it moved from LaGrange to Savannah. Tina was five years older than me and treated me like her little sister, so we immediately connected. She was a fast and experienced runner. I wanted to be like her. Tina asked me to jog with her on the weekend. I accepted the invitation but was afraid I couldn't keep up. I continued to run with her and improved within a few months. She was good for me as I needed to up my game to stay on my scholarship. I did not tell her how much I was struggling in America, but I did tell her that running with her improved my skill. She pulled me through a lot of workouts. I know her goal was to see me succeed. I enjoyed socializing at the training center and got along with all the athletes. We became a family. We encouraged and supported each other. When we had a grievance, we did not complain to the administration. No one wanted to get shipped home. We relied on each other.

Chapter 11

Occasionally, Savannah citizens asked about the program because the sign in front of the building read, "Savannah International Training Center." Sometimes my Zimbabwean-English accent elicited questions about where I was from and why I was in Savannah. On runs, I occasionally met people who wanted to know about the center. A local family invited one of the athletes to their home for the weekend. They decided to host him. Seeing the need for more host families, friends, and neighbors were asked to participate. Many of the host families lived in the same neighborhood. They were all white, but it did not matter. Word spread about the need for host families and hearts opened to us young people, so far from home.

My prayer was answered when Arthur and Candace Peagler volunteered to host me. It was a joy to be in a real home and away from the dormitory. On weekends, when I did not have a scheduled practice or a cross-country competition, I went to their home. Candace was quite a runner and we often jogged together. Arthur was a graduate of Jenkins High School, the school I was attending, and he shared memories of his school days. Marion Peagler, Arthur's mother, "Baba," was a very caring person and I enjoyed helping her with grocery shopping. I never knew my grandparents and became very fond of my "American grandmother." Jordan, the Peagler's daughter, was like a little sister. She was good at soccer and attended Savannah Country Day School. Candace's sister, "Auntie Beth," told me that I lit up a room with my "infectious laugh, positive attitude, free spirit, and open heart." She taught me how to drive. My favorite activities were baseball, kickball, and other games we played in the yard. On one occasion they let me shoot skeet across a pond in the country. Auntie Beth said she could tell I came from a loving family. "Our family was blessed when God brought you into our lives," she said.

Christmas in America was very interesting. Brightly colored lights appeared on all the houses. People went crazy with shopping. At the Peagler's house, I saw my first Christmas tree and was amazed to see so many presents under it. The Peaglers gave me a new pair of shorts with a matching shirt and other articles of clothing. I ate a lot of yummy

Chapter 11

dishes. I had heard of Father Christmas but not Santa Claus. This was all new to me. I knew some Christmas hymns, like "Silent Night," because we sang them in Shona at our church. I missed my family.

I discovered I was not the only student from Africa at my high school. I met Iya Tambe from Cameroon. I invited her to come to the training center to meet other Africans. She and her mother were attending First Presbyterian Church of Savannah and invited me to visit. When Ruth and I visited, we were the only black people in the congregation besides the Tambe family. We were immediately welcomed. John and Ann Tatum, members of the church, offered to give us a ride. They were leaders of a Sunday School class called, "The Timothy Class." Sunday School classes at my Methodist church in Zimbabwe were strictly divided by age, but the Timothy Class invited all ages, although it attracted mostly young adults. I enjoyed being in a Sunday School class again. I felt comfortable enough to participate. They encouraged me to share information about my homeland, and as a member of the class, I was included in social events. Sometimes John and Ann took me out to eat after church. They encouraged and supported me.

Another member of First Presbyterian Church, "Mama Becky," as I call her, invited me to her home to cook sadza and chicken curry. It was my first opportunity to cook sadza in America. We went shopping for the ingredients and I decided to use white ground cornmeal, the closest grain I could find to ground maize at home. Mama Becky provided a pot for boiling water, and I added the cornmeal until I got the right consistency. I also cooked chicken curry and sauce. I showed Mama Becky and her husband Dan how to eat it by scooping up the sadza in one hand, rolling it around, shaping it into a ball, making an indentation using the thumb, and dipping it in chicken curry with sauce. They caught on quickly and we ate our fill. Mama Becky asked many questions about Zimbabwe and its culture because she was sponsoring a boy from Zimbabwe through Child Care, an international program. When she told me the name of the boy I said, "Oh, he is of another tribe." Mama Becky wanted to know how I knew what tribe he was from. "Because of his name," I said. This led to many other questions.

Once I went boating on the inland waterways on the coast of Georgia with Mama Becky, Dan,

Chapter 11

and their niece, Whitney. It was a new experience. I had never seen an ocean up close. It went on and on without end, as far as I could see. I was amazed to see other people were also riding in boats. I was a little afraid of the waves. We stopped and dropped anchor near a little sandy beach. They encouraged me to get into the ocean, which was about three feet deep where we were anchored, but I did not want to. Whitney hopped in the water and demonstrated that it was safe. But in Zimbabwe, dangerous creatures live in rivers and lakes. I was even less sure about oceans. Finally, after much insistence, I slowly inched my way into the water. But I soon got out. I have never lived near an ocean, or any waterway and I did not know how to swim. I was much more comfortable on dry land. I told everybody at the training center about my scary experience with the ocean. Once Mama Becky asked me if I wanted to go on a hike. "A hike?" I asked. "Why would I walk when I can run?" I had walked enough growing up and it certainly was not for fun. We laughed.

Chapter 12

Once I arrived in the United States, I never received any communication directly from the Zimbabwe Olympic Athletics Association or the International Olympic Committee, so I assumed I was to continue training. The Savannah International Training Center coaches entered me in track events. I was a middle to long-distance runner and competed in races from 1500m to 5000/10000m. The 10000m (6.2 mile) race was a bit too long for me. Most of the time we competed as a team, traveling throughout the South. Once I competed in a race held at Savannah State University and local friends cheered me on. It was great to have people come to see me compete.

I slowly came to the realization that I would not be selected to represent Zimbabwe in the 2000 Summer Olympics. No one had to tell me. A female distance runner in Zimbabwe by the name of Samukeliso Moyo represented Zimbabwe in the women's 5000m (3.1 miles). Her personal best was

Running to America

15:40 minutes and mine was 16:40. Julia Sakala ran the ¾ mile (1500m) race. Her best time was 4:07. It also was better than my best time. One day the coaches called George, Norma Jean, and me to the office. We were given a letter from the Zimbabwe Olympic Athletics Association stating our scholarships were not going to be renewed after 1999. I knew the letter was coming and had already started thinking about what I would do. I did not tell my family that my scholarship was ending; I decided to focus on finding an athletic scholarship at a university. I thought I might be a good recruit for college and university track teams. Other athletes were doing the same.

As my high school graduation approached, Ann Tatum gave me a wonderful gift. She took me shopping for the upcoming prom and bought me a long sparkly dress with a side split. It was beautiful. I would not have had a dress for the prom had she not bought one for me. On June 1st, 1999, I graduated from high school. It was my first educational milestone in America. A few days before the event, I picked up my gown, cap, and tassel. I invited everyone I knew to come and help me celebrate. The ceremony, held at the Savannah Civic Center, was filled with families and friends who cheered as we marched in wearing our robes and caps. It was

Chapter 12

thrilling. I was the oldest student in the class, soon to turn 21, but I didn't care. "You have done it," I told myself. I alone knew the sacrifice and work it had taken to achieve the milestone. As my name was called, I nervously walked across the stage and received my diploma. After the ceremony, friends gathered around me. I had a big smile on my face. It was the best experience of my life up to that point.

The Savannah International Training Center's Board of Directors voted to close the center at the end of November 1999 for lack of financial support. The International Olympic Committee had committed on several occasions to send at least twenty-five athletes to the training center, the minimum number needed to break even financially. However, the center was consistently short of the minimum number. Only eighteen athletes remained. The IOC maintained it never planned to be the only source of revenue. There was no choice but to close the center.

Our coaches suggested we apply for admission to colleges if we wanted to stay in the country. I did not want to return home. Even though I missed my family, an opportunity to further my education would not come again if I went home. I could only remain in America if I obtained a student visa. Student visas provided that foreign students could only work on campus, and no more than twenty hours a week. Since I had no financial resources, my only option was to obtain a full collegiate scholarship to pay for my living expenses as well as tuition.

One of the host families assisted an athlete at the center in applying for a full scholarship to Fort Valley State University, a historically black university in Fort Valley, Georgia. She received the scholarship, so I decided to apply and was told that I received a scholarship as well. I packed my bags and moved to the campus, excited to begin a new chapter of my life. At last I was going to college and would compete on a collegiate track team. After a few weeks I was astonished to learn the information given to me was incorrect and no scholarship funds had ever been allocated for me. I was frantic. What was I going to do? I called friends from the training center. I learned that Morris Brown University in Atlanta, another historically black school, had scholarships available. I applied, was accepted, and moved to that campus. Once again, I was told I did not have funding for a scholarship. I was confused and frustrated. The college coaches were not communicating with the financial aid offices. I became increasingly desperate. I might be deported if I did not get accepted

Chapter 12

soon. I called George, my countryman. He gave me updates on options for scholarships circulating among our contacts. Leontine Tsiba, a track athlete from the Congo, suggested I contact Life University in Marietta, Georgia. Once again, I talked with the track coach. I was invited to tour the campus and within a week I received a call offering me a full scholarship. This time I made a lot of inquiries, especially with the financial aid department to be sure the scholarship was fully funded. It was. Coach Rana Reider welcomed me to the program, and I began attending classes and working out with the women's track team. My stress level went down considerably. I finally had a valid student visa and was eager to enter collegiate competitions.

I moved into an apartment on campus. It was much less noisy than life in dormitories. The athletes on the team came from many countries including Kenya, Burundi, Jamaica, Israel, Sweden, and France. We formed quite a diverse and international group. The scholarship provided an allowance for food and the Kenyan athletes gave me rides to a grocery store. I was able to cook my own food, but it did not taste right because the vegetables were not as fresh as the ones grown on our farm and I lacked spices that flavored certain dishes. One of my roommates cooked chicken with peanut sauce and shared it with me. It was delicious. I rarely had the opportunity to cook once I left home and I wasn't really motivated to do so. Sometimes I helped pay for food we cooked as a group. If I did not cook, I tried to be helpful by cutting up vegetables and cleaning the kitchen after meals. I became close friends with many of my teammates. We formed an international community and helped each other overcome loneliness.

The college campus was much bigger than the high school campus I had attended. College professors and instructors left class attendance up to the students. They expected students to be mature enough to make their own decisions. Classes were smaller and the ratio of teacher to students was great. When I was unable to attend class due to traveling with the track team, I made sure I received assignments so I would not fall behind academically. I was treated like an adult and felt very independent. The first-year courses were general core classes. I took Math, English, Computer Science, and Psychology. I received credit in Physical Education for participation on the track team. I worked for twenty hours in the campus bookstore and the library for income. I sent most of it home to my parents, proud that I could help them.

Chapter 13

Life University was a member of the National Association of Intercollegiate Athletics (NAIA) and offered me a great opportunity to begin my collegiate track career. I qualified to compete in distance running—the 3000m, 5000m, and cross-country. I was not competitive in the shorter runs and sprints. Distance running was my strongest category. The NAIA is a smaller conference than the well-known National Collegiate Athletics Association. NCAA member institutions are divided into three divisions. Sometimes our team raced against NCAA athletes in Division I and Division II schools, so we were competing against the best collegiate runners in our conference.

Coach Rana Reider worked with me and individualized my practice runs to maximize my skills. He gave me structured written workout plans and charts for each day. My cross-country runs changed weekly and consisted of practice runs to get used to maintaining a certain speed. Closer to the track meet, the workouts were designed to pick up the pace at the start or end of the race working on both speed and endurance. It included running up and down hills and over varied terrain. Sometimes I ran on the nearby Chattahoochee River Trail. Rest days and easy runs were built in. Coach observed me every day and pointed out ways for me to improve my run. I was constantly learning and improving my skills.

The track meets against NCAA Division I and II teams increased our ability to excel in the NAIA competitions. We traveled to Clemson University, North Carolina State, Georgia Tech, the University of Georgia, Georgia Southern University, the University of Tennessee, and the University of Florida. We won the 2000 NAIA Outdoor Track and Field National Championships and were runners-up in the 2000 NAIA Indoor Track and Field National Championships. I was a six-time All-American NAIA track athlete and the only female cross-country runner at Life University qualified to compete in the NAIA Nationals in 2000. I placed 19th out of 248 runners. I was at the top of my game.

Suddenly, in September 2000, we were stunned to learn that Coach Reider accepted a job as an assistant women's track and field coach at Clemson University. We were suddenly without a coach. Mike

Chapter 13

Spino, the men's coach for track and cross-country, stepped in and helped with the women's distance running program, but it was not the same as having a coach dedicated to the women's team. Coach Spino did not provide me with any workout plans and I had no clue how to structure my own. He just told us to go out for long runs and to stretch when the run ended. I began running with the Kenyan men who were distance runners. On the practice runs I fell behind, but my skills improved.

However, with no dedicated women's track coach, I was not happy and felt increasingly insecure. As the months rolled by with no news about a new women's coach, I became stressed and anxious. With Coach Reider, I felt secure knowing my scholarship remained in effect. When he left and no other coach came along, I feared my scholarship might be terminated. It was difficult to practice on my own and to enter competitions with no one to advise me. I needed a one-on-one relationship with a coach if I was going to further my career. Without Coach Reider, I was floundering without any guidance or plan as to how to move forward. I did not know what might become of the women's team. There was no one to talk to. I had to do something.

I decided to reach out to Coach Wayne Phipps at the University of Idaho, who knew of me through my Zimbabwean countryman, Tawanda Chiwira. Chiwira ran track at the University of Idaho and was a speedster on the track specializing in the 400-meter race. He mentioned my name as a possible asset for the University of Idaho cross-country team. When Coach Phipps first contacted me, I was at the Savannah Training Center and unsure of my future. At the time I did not respond to his communication. I now let Coach Phipps know I was interested in the UI program because I was without a women's track coach. He responded right away and scheduled an official visit for me to come in December 2000. I flew to Spokane, Washington, and Coach Phipps met me at the airport. It was snowing. We rode south for about an hour to the campus in Moscow, Idaho, located along the border with Washington State. All I saw was miles upon miles of open land covered with snow. Moscow was a small city with a beautiful university campus. It was winter break and most of the students were gone.

Coach Phipps gave me a tour of the campus. I visited the Kibbie Dome where the athletic

Chapter 13

department offices were located and met a few administrators on campus. Coach drove me past the places where the track team worked out both indoor and outdoor. We drove past dorms and the student center. I shared my career goals with Coach Phipps, and he appeared ready to provide me with the tools I needed to succeed in my running career. On campus, I talked with Tawanda Chiwira and with Tuelo Setswamorago from Botswana. I knew Tuelo from competitions at World Cross-Country events. I also met Althea Belgrave, from Barbados. They all seemed happy to be at the University of Idaho.

I liked what I learned about the track and field program. Coach Phipps put a very good scholarship offer on the table. I wanted to get back to a structured program with a coach to guide my career. I believed that UI had what I wanted and needed. Best of all, UI competed as a Division I member of the NCAA and Big Sky Conference. I would be training with the best. But the snow! I just kept thinking about the snow and wind and the isolation of the campus. I must admit that I did not like being in a place with so much snow in the winter. However, I knew there was an indoor track program during the winter months and I liked Coach Wayne Phipps and the other

Running to America

coaches I met. They impressed me as being very professional and devoted to the athletes and the track program. As I thought about my situation, I was conflicted. Moving to the Pacific Northwest all the way across the country was a big decision. Moving from university to university had not worked out for me. I began losing weight and was emotionally drained. I had no one to advise me. I was concerned about losing my student visa. I was too stubborn to call my friends and get their input. The university campus was closed for the holidays, so I decided to go home.

Chapter 14

When I traveled to the United States in March 1997, the International Olympic Association provided me with a round-trip ticket. I decided to use the original return ticket to travel home. I bought a new ticket to travel from Zimbabwe back to the U.S. with money I carefully set aside from my Life University stipend and packed my bag. I called my family and gave them the good news.

My friend Tina Paulino drove me to the Atlanta airport. She was excited for me. I did not know what to expect when I arrived. Would anyone in my family be at the airport? Would my parents look different? Could I slip back into speaking Shona after so many years of speaking English? Would my father be proud of me? Would my parents think I had changed? Had I changed? Thoughts flooded over me as the hours passed on the many legs of my trip home. I was physically exhausted. But when the wheels hit the runway in Harare, my energy level shot up. As I walked off the plane, I saw my father, mother, some of my siblings, and members of my extended family. How had they gotten to the airport? I didn't care. I rushed over and gave my father a big hug. Hugging is an American custom. My father was not prepared for it. He pulled away quickly, not used to being touched in that manner. How could I have forgotten? It was just my excitement. My mother and I hugged, and she did not let go, tears of joy running down her face. My family welcomed me, probably wondering who this new Letiwe was. It was the best welcome I ever received.

The heat suddenly hit me. It was summer in Zimbabwe. Why did I wear a sweater? What was I thinking? People I recognized looked older, some slimmer. "I was too thin," they said. "Why was I not eating enough?" they asked. "I am training much more than I did before," I said. "It keeps me thin." "Your Shona accent is different," they said. I did not understand. I was speaking the way I always had. We rode to my aunt and uncle's house in Harare for lunch. My parents said a prayer, thanking God for my safe arrival and for allowing us to see each other again. After lunch, we began the long trip to our village. I looked out the window. Everything looked different. My mother had many questions. "Did I like America?" "What was it like?" "Was I

Chapter 14

going back or was I home for good?" I probably had not explained everything clearly before coming home. "I am visiting for a few weeks and then I will go back," I said. "I need to finish my education." I did not tell my parents about the troubles I faced. They did not need to worry about me.

The homestead was run down and looked worse than when I left. I was heartbroken at its condition and with the realization that I did not have enough money to help renovate it. The next big wind or rainstorm could easily destroy it and I feared for their lives. My father killed a cow to feed the many family members that came home for Christmas. It was a dear cost to my family. When the beef was boiled and cooked over a fire, it was delicious and tasted like home. On Christmas Day, we went to church and the pastor announced my return. Church members gathered around me to welcome me home. My father invited relatives in the village to come to the house so we could celebrate. He said it was the best Christmas ever. His errant daughter was home.

The days rushed by. As I began to organize my things for the return trip home, I discovered my return airline ticket was missing from my purse. I looked everywhere. I frantically asked everyone if they had seen it. This was a disaster. How was

Running to America

I going to get back to America? No one in my family had money to pay for an airplane ticket to the United States. I had planned to leave a little money for my parents when I left and hurriedly counted the money in my wallet. I found a phone at the market and called British Airways. They told me my name was listed on the computer as a passenger for the flight. A paper ticket had been issued to me. They could not issue another one, and I needed to show a ticket to get a boarding pass. That meant that I was going to have to buy another ticket. I rode a bus for hours to Harare and took a taxi to the British Airways ticket office. To my relief, I had just enough money to pay for a ticket. To this day I do not know who took the ticket or why. What if my cash had also been taken? My life in America would have come to a sudden end. It was that serious. No bank would have given me a loan. It would have been hopeless. Shaken from this experience, I packed for my trip back to America. Before I left, my father said a prayer for my safety. I said goodbye to my family once again. I did not know when I would be able to return. It was the last time I saw my father.

Chapter 15

When I returned to the States, I decided to stay at Life University to see if a new women's track coach came along. I did not want to move to Idaho in the middle of winter. I continued my scholarship at Life University for the 2001 winter and spring quarters. Even though we had no coach for the women's team, we did our best and supported each other. In 2001 we again won the NAIA Outdoor Track and Field National competition.

Finally, I gave up on Life University and called Coach Phipps. I told him I would come to the University of Idaho in August. He was happy with my decision. As the spring 2001 quarter winded down, I talked with Coach Mike Spino, coach of the men's track team, and told him that I planned to transfer to the University of Idaho. He was extremely opposed to the idea. The cross-country women's track program at Life University would suffer. I was the top female distance runner at the time. He told me he was recruiting more women athletes and counting on me for another good season. It seemed to me that the track program was all about collegiate standing for him and had nothing to do with me personally. He had no interest in my career. If Coach Spino had worked with me and provided me with structured workouts I would not have considered a transfer. But he did not. I never expected to be given special treatment, but I did expect to have a coach. I decided that my future lay at the University of Idaho with coaches who would challenge me and guide my track career.

I went to the Register's Office and requested my transcript be sent to UI. I had a good grade average, above what was required for a scholarship. I completed an application to UI and sent the required documentation. I met with the International Program Office to be sure they updated my student visa status in the computer system. Somewhere in the middle of all the paperwork, I learned that I needed a release form signed by Coach Spino, releasing me from the Life University track program. I thought the release form was a routine matter. It was not. I did not read NAIA procedures and rules; no one told me the significance of the form. The NAIA regulations provided that the coach had sole authority to make the decision to release an athlete. Coach Spino decided not to sign a release. However,

Chapter 15

as the weeks went by and my plans didn't change, I talked again with Coach Spino. My understanding when I left was that he would fax a release form when I enrolled at the University of Idaho.

In August 2001 I moved to Moscow, Idaho. The University of Idaho Vandals were the intercollegiate athletic teams representing the school. They competed as a NCAA Division I member in the Big Sky Conference, later joining the Big West Conference. The weather was much better than my first visit. Coach Wayne Phipps told me he would contact Coach Spino and see when the release form would be faxed. I was hopeful the matter would be resolved quickly. After all, I was on the other side of the country and the two schools did not compete against each other. More importantly, I was an international student and my eligibility to stay in the United States with a student visa was based on my enrollment as a student. If I did not compete as an athlete, I would not be offered a scholarship. Without a scholarship, I had no funds to attend a university. My visa would be revoked, and I would have to return to Zimbabwe. I did not think that would happen. I was optimistic… or maybe just naive.

I began training with the women's team and attended classes. It felt good to be working with a coach again. I was issued a uniform, workout clothes, track shoes, and equipment. The first meet was hosted by the University of Idaho a few weeks after I arrived. I was entered to run the cross-country race. On the day of the cross country meet, I was at the starting line when Coach Phipps walked over and took me out of the lineup. He had bad news. He thought Coach Spino would fax a release form that day, but he did not. Not that day or any following day. Therefore, I was not allowed to compete. I was "redshirted." The NAIA rules stated that without a release, I would have to wait a year before being allowed to compete in collegiate track. I could not even practice with the team. I was completely shut out.

Walking away from the starting line, I tried to hide my emotions from Coach Phipps and my teammates. It was humiliating. I felt like throwing up. I left the cross country course, went to my room, and cried. It was the worst day of my life. My head ached. All my training was for nothing. My career was over. The rule regarding a release probably discouraged athletes from shopping around from school to school. In my case, however, I do not think it served as a deterrence to anyone. No one

Chapter 15

told me I could have challenged his decision. It did not matter. I believed I had no recourse.

It took me a few days to come to terms with the news. I thought about my decision to leave Life University. Over the next few days, I gradually concluded that I made the right choice, no matter the consequences. I felt strongly that Coach Phipps was the right coach for me. After being redshirted for a year, I would come back stronger than ever. Then I panicked. Would I have to leave school? Would my scholarship end? Where would I go? What would I do? Once again, I had to hope that God would take care of me.

Chapter 16

I was not thrown out of UI and my scholarship was not terminated. Coach Phipps decided to stick by me and in return, I promised him that I would stay at UI until I graduated. We both kept our word. During the year I was redshirted, my scholarship paid for my tuition, books, room and board, and other necessities. As a student, I could maintain my F-1 academic student visa and was allowed to work twenty hours a week on campus—so I worked in the bookstore. I felt bad living on UI's money. I was unable to give anything in return. I studied hard and received good grades. I decided to major in Business, focusing on Marketing and Human Resource Management.

Coach Phipps worked up practice runs for me, and I trained on my own harder than ever. He drove me to different locations so I could train on varying terrains. Even though I could not compete for UI, I could enter races as an individual. That enabled me to see how I performed in relation to the UI team members and other teams. Sometimes I watched the UI women's distance running team compete and inwardly groaned. If I had been on the team, I could have contributed my talent and we might have won. It was so frustrating.

Coach Phipps suggested that with my speed and endurance, I might be good at the steeplechase. The steeplechase is a distance race that requires runners to leap over barriers, including barriers with small pools of water eight to ten feet long. It is like the equestrian steeplechase but run by athletes. It seemed dangerous. If I fell or slipped while jumping, I might break a bone or twist a muscle. My only experience in jumping over a hurdle was at the Hande Primary School where the high jump was part of our track and field events. At Hande, we pounded two sticks into the ground and then balanced one stick on top. I tried the high jump but usually fell on the ground. The high jump was not for me.

At Coach's urging I gave the steeplechase a try. Coach Phipps adjusted the height of the hurdles from 36 inches for men to 30 inches for women. At 5'6" I found I could clear the hurdles without too much effort. The race was 7.5 laps around the track with 28 hurdles. Coach and I went to the track at Washington State University where I

Chapter 16

practiced the water jumps. I entered myself in the Boise State University Women's Steeplechase. At the beginning of the race, we were spread out in a horizontal line. After about 50 meters, we could cross over lanes. My strategy was to position myself to have a clear view and to adjust my stride as I approached the barriers. As I came to each water barrier, I felt a sense of anxiety, knowing that any misstep could lead to a fall. At the same time, I felt a sense of anticipation and excitement as I cleared each obstacle, knowing I was one hurdle closer to the finish line. The top of the barrier was about 15cm or six inches wide. I adjusted my stride so I could land with one foot on the top of the barrier and push off over the water. I never did completely clear it and one or both of my feet always got wet. I fell at one of the water jumps but quickly got up and continued running. I remember the race as one of my worst, but to my surprise, I won! My time qualified me for the Women's NCAA Steeplechase. That meant I could compete in the steeplechase for UI the next year. I had to admit, Coach Phipps knew I could run the steeplechase, but he had to convince me I could do it. It confirmed my belief that with the right coach, I was capable of excelling beyond my expectations. The steeplechase eventually became my favorite event.

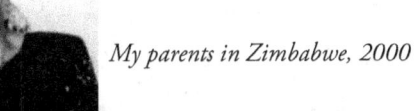
My parents in Zimbabwe, 2000

Coach Chikoto with me at the Harare airport, 1994

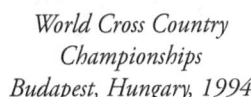

World Cross Country Championships Budapest, Hungary, 1994

Dorowa Track Club, Zimbabwe, 1994 (Me second from right and coach Chikoto top center)

Coach Chikoto in his office before taking me to airport, 1994

Big West cross-country champions, Vandals, 2002

With Norma-Jean Harry in LaGrange, GA, 1997

HS Graduation with Becky in Savannah, 1999

Steeplechase race Sacramento, CA, 2003

With Coach Phipps @ NCAA Outdoor Nationals, 2003

West Region Cross Country race, 2004

Photo of Kyle that I fell in love with, 2008

*Our wedding day
Bremerton, WA, 2009*

With Tina Papaya at my wedding, Bremerton, WA, 2009

Wedding party Bremerton, WA, 2009

Gogo and Mother Patton in Zimbabwe, 2011

Kyle and Gogo in Zimbabwe, 2011

My brothers George and Albert, Zimbabwe 2011

With Ann and John Tatum, Savannah, GA, 2011

US citizenship ceremony, California, 2013

My brother Darlington, Zimbabwe, 2014

My brother Albert at my mother's homestead, 2014

My mother carrying Caryn, Zimbabwe, 2014

With my sisters and mother at my mother's homestead L to R: Jenipher, Emma, me, mother, and Tabeth, 2014

With my niece Chipo and her husband Gideon and my brother Israel (far right) South Africa, 2014

The homestead showing my mother's round kitchen room and the main house. The home was upgraded with new roofing in 2015

Gidion and Chipo Munyaradzi, South Africa, 2021

Itayi Mutandi and Kyle at Harare airport, 2022

Caryn carrying a water bucket in Zimbabwe, 2023

Alexander and Caryn with Gogo on her farm, Zimbabwe, 2023

Caryn and Alexander holding their Gogo's chickens at the homestead in Zimbabwe, 2023

With my mother on her farm, Zimbabwe, 2023

My mother working hard on her farm, 2023

*Caryn in Shona class
Zimbabwe, 2023*

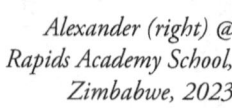

*Alexander (right) @
Rapids Academy School,
Zimbabwe, 2023*

*With Coach Abdi Bile,
Savannah, 2023*

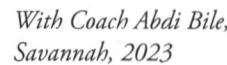

*My sister Emma (center) playing
the drum at her church in
Zimbabwe, 2024*

Savannah International Training Center Athletes Reunion, Savannah, GA 2023

With Ruth Mansogo (L) and Tina Paulino (R) at the Savannah reunion, 2023

Chapter 17

In the summer of 2002, I began training with the team. My year of redshirting was over. I was ready to release my pent-up anger and frustration. Not only had I survived, but I also now qualified for the steeplechase, in addition to other distance race categories. In the fall of 2002, I proudly wore the Vandals jersey. I went on early morning runs and endured grueling workouts. I did not want Coach Phipps to regret his decision to put me on the team. Stepping up to the starting line, I was ready physically and mentally. At our home meet I won and broke the school record in the 4k cross-country. Over the next few months, I was named Athlete of the Week several times. As the season continued, our women's distance team excelled. UI captured the team title. At home meets, students and teachers came to cheer us on.

Coming into the 2002 Big West Cross Country Championships, the University of Idaho was predicted to either win or be in second place. The competition that year was held in California at UC Riverside and included ten collegiate teams, with the University of California Santa Barbara defending the title and favored to win again.

Coach Phipps was the kind of coach who knew exactly how to motivate us; he took the time to speak with each of us individually before the race. I think he was aware that deep down I struggled with self-confidence, but he knew my potential and was able to encourage me without adding undue pressure: "Letiwe," he said, "You have worked so hard; you've been to quite a few of these cross-country races…University of Washington, University of Oregon…and you've been winning! Look at how you've been performing…you are equipped to do better than anyone else in this race."

After he spoke with us individually, he and the coaching staff gathered the team for a meeting in the hotel the night before the race. Cross-country is a team effort, and the more runners who place high in the race, the better the team's overall chances of winning. Coach made sure we knew he was counting on every one of us to do our best and work together.

We all circled up for Coach's pep talk: "This is it. We have worked so hard to be where we are right now. There's nothing to lose now. Everyone

Chapter 17

out there is also scared of you guys! We are the underdog, I get it, but at the end of the day anything can happen, the team that is predicted to win might not win! Let's get out there and do what we do and do our best. Now bring it in…"

He extended his arm forward and we all followed with our cheer: "1 -2 -3…VANDALS!"

On the morning of the 5K race, my teammates circled up at the starting line for a prayer and words of encouragement for one another. "We got this," said one. "Let's go, Vandals," said another. "Let's take the title away," I added, which caused the girls to give me a surprised glance all at once. Talking was unusual for me; I was normally quiet before a race. I found it useful to use all my energy to focus inward and prepare mentally.

Coach suggested right before the start that I not lead the pack; he thought I should hang back a bit and feel out the competition.

We lined up, I set my sights forward, took one final deep breath, and BAM! The race was on.

At the 2K mark I was feeling good, but the leader of the pack, a runner from UCSB, was going too slow; she and I were at the front and I could feel her breath on my right shoulder. I took one step back and realized we were alternating the lead; when she created too much of a gap, I would speed up. Midway through the race, I began doubting myself: if I take off, I might burn out and she's gonna beat me…

With 1K to go, I started seeing her slowing down. Coach yelled from the sideline: "This is it, Letiwe! Now 1K to go- let's get going!" Coach was famous for giving us updates on the overall race at each lap, and this was his moment: he knew one of my biggest strengths was on the hills. The final loop had a 100+ meter uphill grade. I started picking up the pace and noticed she was starting to slowly fall behind me. I can't count on this yet because I have another 500 meters to go, I thought, but at the same time I could tell I was done with her. I started running my own race at that moment and competing only against myself. 200 meters to the finish there was another 50 meter hill; I looked back and realized there was no way she would catch me.

I crossed the finish line, arms wide in the air, my heart pounding with joy! I turned and ran back to cheer on my teammates—excited to see two or three in the top ten. Coach was at the finish line before the scores were even out; he was telling everyone around him, "We got this! We got the team title!" We were all jumping, cheering and hugging, tears and laughter rolling up strong into

Chapter 17

that California sky.

Coach had a feeling we were going to win the title. He had invited his parents to travel from Canada for the meet. It was a big victory for the University of Idaho Vandals. On top of that, I won Big West Conference Athlete of the Year, and Coach Phipps won Big West Conference Coach of the Year. It was a triple win for the UI cross-country team. The Vandals online website said, "UI Women win Big West Cross Country Championship by Seven Points Over Second-Place UC Santa Barbara." "Sophomore Letiwe Marakurwa made it a clean sweep for the Vandals." Coach Phipps said, "Letiwe ran in control the whole time." It was the first time the UI women's cross-country team won the title. It was a historic moment made even sweeter by the support we received from the community.

In the span of one year, my emotions had turned from deep despair to pure joy. My hard work and determination to excel paid off. I was so happy that Coach Phipps won Coach of the Year because he took a chance on me. I will always be grateful for his support.

With my training for the steeplechase, I qualified for the NCAA Division I Track and Field Championships in Sacramento, California, and became the first woman UI distance runner to

Running to America

qualify for the NCAA D1 championships in the 3000m Women's Steeplechase. In early June 2003, I finished first in the 3,000m steeplechase preliminaries at the NCAA Outdoor Track and Field Championships in Sacramento, California. "She ran a great race," Head Coach Wayne Phipps said. "Just kind of stayed behind, took the lead with a lap to go and destroyed everybody. She only ran hard for the last 200 meters. It looks pretty good for her to be in the top three or so." At the final NCAA Championships in Sacramento, I ran like the wind. At the finish line, I had no feeling in my legs. I was 4th place overall and broke my own record at 9:52.98.

When I was named All-American in the women's 3000m steeplechase, it meant I was among the top athletes in the country. I set a record for the Big West Conference and the University of Idaho. Proud to represent my school on a national stage, I was at the height of my collegiate career. Zimbabwe did not compete in the women's 3000m steeplechase category at that time, so technically I became the first Zimbabwean woman to hold a record in that category.

At the 2003 Big West outdoor track and field championships, I won the 3000m steeplechase, the 10000m, and the following day I was third overall

Chapter 17

in the 5000m race. It was run in less than 24 hours, but Coach had prepared me, and I knew I could do it. In 2004, I was again undefeated in the 3000m steeplechase, setting the pace from the start to the finish. I also ran the 5000m and the 10000m and finished 4th and 2nd respectively.

When I was not training or competing, I enjoyed being with students outside the world of track. One of my friends was Native American and lived on the nearby Nez Perce Reservation. He was an outdoor person and liked fishing and hunting. I attended a Pow-Wow and ate frybread and Indian tacos. Our cultures were similar in some respects, like the gathering of people to sing, play drums and other instruments. We biked around campus and on trails. Occasionally we went out to eat. Once we traveled with friends to snow ski in Coeur D'Alene, Idaho. I did not know how to snow ski and did not try, but I enjoyed the company and beautiful scenery. I dated some of the guys who were on the UI track team, but our hectic schedules prevented spending much time together. Occasionally I had friends over to my apartment for dinner and they reciprocated. CJ's nightclub in downtown Moscow was a favorite place for students to hang out and socialize and I enjoyed going with friends. I did not drink alcohol but played pool and danced. Sometimes I went to student union-sponsored events.

In Savannah, Mama Becky kept up with my track career by reading about the Vandals on the University of Idaho website. I also sent her emails with a link to news when I was featured. The athletic news roundup for the week always started with the rousing UI fight song, "Go Vandals Go," accompanied by the band. At work, Mama Becky decided to click on the link I sent her. The UI fight song began blaring through her computer sound system, disturbing the peace of her quiet office. People from adjacent offices came running over to see what the music was all about. I guess I was famous for the day. I thought it was very funny. It was the last time Mama Becky clicked on a link I sent her while she was at work. That summer Mama Becky and Dan came by to visit me during their travel west. They were my first visitors in Idaho, and it meant the world to me. I showed them around the beautiful campus and the places I trained. In my apartment, Mama Becky saw about 10 pairs of worn running shoes lined up on a shelf. She decided it needed documenting and took pictures of it. She was laughing because she remembered a time when I refused to wear track shoes at all.

Chapter 17

Now I had a crazy number of shoes.

In the Christmas season of 2003, I traveled to Savannah for a visit and stayed with Mama Becky and Dan. It was nice to be back in Savannah. I visited with a few friends from the training center days. We talked nonstop, excited to reconnect. John and Ann Tatum and Mama Becky and Dan took me out to eat one night at a nice restaurant. On New Year's Day, Mama Becky encouraged me to participate in a New Year's event called the "Tybee Polar Plunge." It took place at the local beach on Tybee Island. I was not sure I understood this custom, but I decided to give it a try. Every New Year's Day hundreds of brave people wearing bathing suits and costumes line up on the beach and, when given the "Go" signal, run screaming into the ocean waves. Within seconds most run right back out because it is so cold! I wore a Santa hat and my bathing suit under my coat. At the signal, I took off my coat and bravely ran into the water. Like most, I quickly turned around and came right back. Mama Becky had a towel waiting for me. There are some crazy customs in America.

Back on campus, I began training for the 2004 track season. I was in my senior year. I never liked racing indoors, and with that mentality, I never made it to the indoor national competition. When the outdoor competition began, I qualified for nationals in the 3000m steeplechase. The event was held in Austin, Texas. I was used to cold and moderate weather in Idaho. I had not lived in the southern part of the country for years and had forgotten about the humidity and repressive heat of the summertime. It was unbearable and I did not do well. I came in 13th overall in the preliminary race and failed by one second to qualify for the final competition. I was so angry. I let down my coach and team. I put too much pressure on myself and did not realize how much stress affected me and my teammates. It was disappointing. However, I finished my collegiate outdoor distance running year knowing I gave it all I had. More importantly, I made it to the NCAA D1 outdoor championships. It was a great way to wrap up my collegiate track career at the University of Idaho.

Chapter 18

I graduated from UI with two B.S. degrees in Marketing and Human Resource Management. What was I going to do now? I did not have a plan. I explored my eligibility as a foreign national for an H-1B temporary skilled worker visa. The visa was intended to help American firms address labor shortages in rapidly growing fields that demanded specialized skills. There was a shortage of nurses in the country. I looked at the requirements for a degree in nursing and found I had taken very few of the required courses needed to qualify. I entered my name in the national green card lottery but winning was a super long shot. I could apply to serve in the United States Army. The military offered a path to citizenship. I was physically in great shape. But it was a route only open if I had a green card giving me permanent residence. I did not qualify. I realized I had skills I could apply toward being a track and field coach even though coaching was not a specialized skill. Why not pursue it? If that was my goal, I needed to get a master's degree. UI offered a Master of Science in Sports and Recreation Management. With a graduate degree, maybe I could become a coach and an instructor at a school. I could continue to stay in America with my student visa.

I applied for the graduate program at UI, was accepted, and began taking coursework in January 2005. I was granted a F-1 student visa. I worked as an assistant coach for the track and cross country team and in return, my tuition was paid. Tuition was more expensive for international students. Without payment for tuition and fees, I could not afford to remain in school. I went on practice runs with the team and traveled to meets. The job allowed me to stay in shape so I could compete in races beyond the college level. It was not easy simultaneously being a student, an assistant coach, and an athlete in training. The graduate courses were demanding. Sometimes my eyes burned from staring at the computer screen for hours. I had to pass all my courses to stay eligible for the student visa. My stomach growled because I did not take time to eat. I relied on tea to keep me going. My life was a never-ending cycle of schoolwork, coaching,

Chapter 18

and training. I had many sleepless nights.

During a break, I traveled to Atlanta to visit friends from the Savannah Training Center who were living in the Atlanta area. I stayed with my friend Ruth Mangue Mansogo who was married with three children. It was nice to be with Ruth again. I saw teammates Ngozi Asinga from Zambia and Tommy Asinga from Suriname who met and married. My friends Ousman Diarra and Abderaman Brahim visited with me, and I talked to numerous friends by phone. It was a much-needed break.

During the 2006 school winter break, Fanta Ceesay, from Gambia, West Africa, invited me to visit her in Seattle, Washington. I knew Fanta from the Savannah Training Center where she trained as a sprinter. She liked the Seattle area and said if I wanted to move there, she would open her door for me. What a great offer. She had a car and gave me a driving tour. Seattle had a diverse population, and I met several Africans living in the area. The opportunity for employment seemed promising. I decided to keep Seattle open as an option.

I applied to the U.S. Citizenship and Immigration Services for permanent residence. It was denied. My Immigrant Petition for Alien Worker was denied as well. I wasn't seeking asylum so that category was not an option. I learned about a student work visa called Optional Practical Training. It allowed F-1 academic students to work in the United States for up to 12 months after graduation from college or graduate school to gain practical experience in their field of study. To be eligible for an OPT work visa, I had to complete my degree and work for a year maintaining my F-1 student status. I went to the International Program Office at the UI and spoke with the Director of the International students. She reviewed my file and told me I qualified for the OPT visa. I applied and was approved. I was able to work off campus for the first time. I found a job working with my friend Sheila Lemuta at an assisted living facility for a few months while I finished my graduate degree. If I was going to qualify as a coach, I knew it was important to be certified by the National Council for Accreditation of Coaching Education in USA Track & Field. I took a course to prepare for the exam. The course covered fundamental rules, safety, and risk management and prepared individuals to coach at the junior age, high school, and club division level. The exam was only given in select cities, so I flew to Chicago to take the exam. I passed and

Chapter 18

received a USATF Level 1 certification.

In May 2007 I received my graduate degree. I was proud of my academic achievement. But what was next in my life? I had been a student on campus for almost seven years. Reality began to set in. I was now on my own financially, with no scholarship to support me and no job offers. I was no longer a part of an athletic track team. There was no foreseeable opportunity to train for competitive distance running. Part of me wanted to move back to the Atlanta, Georgia area where I had contacts. Part of me wanted to go back to Zimbabwe. I was homesick. Unfortunately, I did not have the resources to visit my parents in Zimbabwe. What I did have was a work authorization from the OPT program.

I remembered Fanta's offer and called her to see if it was still open. It was. Seattle was not far from Moscow. I moved in with Fanta in her one-bedroom apartment in Everett, Washington, a city less than thirty miles north of Seattle. The big city was exciting. Fanta worked for AT&T at a customer care call center from 5 am to 2 pm. Using my work visa, I applied for the same position and was hired. Since Fanta had a car, we were able to carpool. The job required talking to customers, the majority of whom were very unhappy and angry about charges on their bills. My role was to resolve their concerns. I did not like the job. My African-English accent was not understood. It was frustrating because the primary purpose of the job was to be effective in communicating. The pay was not so good either. Within a few months, Fanta began working a different shift and was no longer able to give me a ride to work. Public buses did not travel the route I needed. There was only one solution—I needed a car.

Fanta and I went to a car dealership and looked for cheap cars. I found a used Chevy Impala and purchased it. I thought I could afford the monthly payments on the car, but my estimate was wrong. I needed to find a job that paid more money, so I took a position with Verizon at a customer call center. It did not pay much more than AT&T but I liked my manager and the other employees.

Fanta and I looked for a two-bedroom apartment. We found one and moved in. Soon, however, Fanta took in her older sister and her child. We found a three-bedroom apartment, moved in and everyone had their own space. We split the rent, utility bills, and food. Fanta was a great cook as was her sister. They cooked fish, chicken, meat pies, and pepper soup and taught me how to cook their recipes. I went to a house party one weekend

Chapter 18

where I met other Africans in the area. A friend of Fanta from Gambia asked me out and we began dating. He was finishing his nursing degree at a local college. He took me to the top of the Space Needle in downtown Seattle. We went on a few more dates but after three months I decided to move on. He was not for me in the long run. I had often dreamed of finding a mate and being married by the time I was 26. I was now 29 years old with no prospects for a long-term relationship.

I was pleased I could continue to send money home to my aging parents. I bought calling cards providing for longer amounts of time. I could call home more frequently and not be rushed. I wanted to go home for a visit but did not feel comfortable traveling on my work visa. It allowed me to work in the United States. However, if I traveled to Zimbabwe, I would have to apply for a visa to travel back to America. I knew Africans who went home for a visit and were denied work visas to return to the U.S., even if they had jobs waiting for them. I did not want to risk it.

Chapter 19

Tuelo Setswamorago, my friend from Botswana, told me about eHarmony, an online dating site. She communicated with men online and said I should try it. I was terrified. This was not for me. Bad things happened to women who dated men they met online. Tuelo was insistent. She suggested I pay the small fee for the eHarmony app, and if I did not like it, cancel it. I decided to give it a try. I went online to see what it was about. It was fun and scary at the same time. It became more appealing when I realized eHarmony encouraged long-term relationships. I answered questions about my likes and dislikes, things that motivated me and I began to develop a profile. I posted a few photos. In one photo I wore a colorful African outfit that Fanta had given me. In another, I wore blue jeans and a black spaghetti-striped shirt with my hair nicely done.

I browsed through the application for matches. To my surprise, I was immediately attracted to the profile of one man, Kyle Patton. I loved the picture he posted standing with his motorcycle. It stole my heart away. We cautiously began communicating through the security of eHarmony. Kyle came across as very responsible, independent, and patient. We both had an interest in sports. eHarmony suggested the first in-person meeting be short and take place during the day. Following the safety suggestions, I told Kyle I would meet him for lunch. We decided to meet at a restaurant near my workplace. I waited anxiously in my car until it was time to go in. I recognized Kyle from the profile pictures as he stood by the entrance to the restaurant. During lunch Kyle was quiet. I was very nervous. I tried to begin a conversation. He said very little. Maybe he did not understand me because of my accent. Maybe he had never met anyone from Africa. Maybe he thought I was part of a scam, and I was going to ask for money. Maybe he did not like me. Maybe he was just a quiet person. I ordered. He ordered. I talked. He listened. Was I talking too much? Why wasn't he talking? Was I eating too much? I tried to eat slowly. We were both uncomfortable and our meeting was short, but the first nerve-racking date was over. I relaxed. I was alive and nothing bad had happened to me. Were we going to talk

Chapter 19

again? Were we going on another date? We were.

Kyle was the youngest of five children. His father served in the U.S. Navy and the family moved from place to place. By the time Kyle came along, the family was settled in Bremerton, Washington where he spent his childhood and adolescence. He was fourteen when his father passed away. Kyle went to Brown University in Providence, Rhode Island, and majored in Economics and Psychology. When we met, he was living in Bellevue and working for Microsoft. The Microsoft campus was in Redmond, Washington near his home. Kyle worked in SQL, the Structured Query Language Server group. Kyle explained to me that SQL was looking to create an online database service using their database product which was previously only shipped on disk for people to install and run themselves. He was managing the operations team responsible for the infrastructure setup and management of the running software and service. I did not fully understand his job, but he impressed me when he talked about his career. Not long after we began dating Kyle took me to meet his mother. I loved knowing he valued family as much as I did.

When I told my family I was in love with an American, their first thought was that Kyle was white. I told them Kyle was black, but I most

Running to America

certainly did not tell my parents that I met Kyle online. My mother would have thought I was crazy. It would have been incomprehensible. I could hear her say, "Couldn't you find someone in church, or school, or down the street?" She had no perception of life in America and knew nothing about computers. We were living in very different worlds. My mother was concerned about the news that Kyle did not speak Shona. My father, on the other hand, looked forward to meeting Kyle because he could speak with him in English. He was very proud of his English language skills.

The first time Kyle came to my apartment in Everett, my roommate, Fanta, cooked chicken with seasonings from Gambia. We also cooked meat pies and fish pies. Kyle took me to a few of his favorite restaurants in the Bellevue area. The best dinner date we had was a dinner cruise. We enjoyed the views of the Seattle skyline. Kyle took me to movies, and we both especially loved going to Broadway shows in downtown Seattle. He even took me shopping and bought me clothes. I had little income, and he was very generous. I learned Kyle liked track and was a short distance runner. When he was a student at O'Dea High School in downtown Seattle, his team won the boys 4x100m sprint relay. Kyle wanted to know all about my

Chapter 19

travels to other countries to compete in track and about my experience as an athlete in America. I learned his favorite sport was football. I watched football games with him and even participated in Fantasy Football. I learned about the football weekly athlete line ups, how to bench players, check on my player's performance and make substitutions. Kyle's mom also enjoyed watching football. If we visited her on Sundays, we went to church in the morning and hurried back to her home in time for the first football game of the day.

Kyle loved riding his motorcycle and I enjoyed sitting on the back holding on to him. We rode around neighborhoods near his home. He tried to teach me how to work the motorcycle and took me to the Microsoft campus parking lot to practice. I did not do well. My concern was falling and breaking a bone or damaging his motorcycle. I was not a motorcyclist, but I loved riding with him as the driver. As Kyle and I spent more time together, our conversations became more direct. I grew up in an environment with rigid adherence to gender roles. I told Kyle, "I accept the role of cooking, cleaning, and caring for our home. However, I do not want to be a stay-at-home wife. I want to have a career." Kyle understood and accepted my goal. He knew being an athlete and pursuing a career in track was a significant part of my identity. We both wanted children at some point in our lives. After his father passed away, Kyle and his siblings helped to support their mother. I could relate because I supported my parents. Kyle and I both took charge of our lives at an early age. He was genuinely interested in who I was as a person and not in the status of my family.

Chapter 20

Kyle proposed to me in November 2008, a few months after we met. I was 30 and he was 34. We knew soon after meeting that we were meant for each other. His big family was open and loving and ready to embrace me. And I was not the only foreigner in the family—Kyle's oldest brother's wife was from Turkey and another brother married a woman whose family immigrated to the U.S. from Portugal.

We set our wedding date for August 15, 2009. Kyle's family was Catholic, and I chose to convert to Catholicism. We went to premarital counseling at St. Louis Parish Catholic Church in Bellevue, WA. Kyle and I were busy with our jobs and had little time to plan the event. In stepped my mother-in-law, Mother Patton. She was a great wedding planner and kept the costs from getting out of hand. The wedding took place at Our Lady Star of the Sea in Bremerton, Washington. My friend, Tina Papaya, came from Atlanta and shared a hotel room with me the night before the wedding. She was my makeup artist. I met Tina when I lived in Savannah, and she was like a big sister. She came from Mutare, Zimbabwe, not far from my home. We decided to call my mother. My mother said, "Tina, you must give Letiwe advice about marriage." Tina assured my mother she would represent my family at the wedding and everything would be fine. Tina was a blessing because she spoke Shona and my mother felt included in a small way.

Our wedding was beautiful. My bridesmaids included Kyle's sister, Venetria Patton, my friend Tina Papaya, and my maid of honor, Tuelo Setswamorago, who lived in San Francisco and came to share the experience with me. Kyle's brothers were his groomsmen. Mama Becky and Dan came to the wedding from Savannah, Georgia. I almost cried when I saw them. They were my surrogate parents. John and Ann Tatum sent a lovely gift. Former track teammates and college friends traveled to share in the event. Many attendees knew the Patton family, longtime residents of Bremerton. After the wedding, we celebrated with cake, dancing, speeches, and toasts. It was nice to see Kyle's family and my

Chapter 20

friends enjoying the day; I only wished my family could have witnessed the wedding.

We decided to make our honeymoon a road trip. Kyle rented a Chrysler Sebring convertible and we both fell in love with it. We started in northern California briefly visiting Kyle's brothers. Kyle and I met and married so quickly that there were no opportunities to visit them. I told Kyle's brothers and wives the short version of my life. It would have taken days to tell them more. San Diego was our next stop. Kyle owned a timeshare at the World-Mark Oceanside resort. Our room looked out over the ocean. We ate out and leisurely walked around. We talked about how lucky we were to have found each other. It was worth the wait.

The scenery between California and Las Vegas was breathtaking. I had never seen this part of the country. We stayed at the famous Bellagio Hotel in Las Vegas and went to several shows. We enjoyed riding on the open road, the wind blowing in our faces. Once we came to a road where the speed limit was 80mph. Kyle hit the gas pedal and off we went. He was having fun. Some stretches of the roads were so narrow, I was sure two cars going in opposite directions could not possibly pass. We traveled on roads next to steep slopes. I kept my head down, not wanting to look. I developed a great appreciation for Kyle's driving skills. Two years after our road trip, Kyle bought a new Shelby Mustang.

I moved out of the apartment with Fanta and in with Kyle. We both returned to work. Our home in Bellevue, Washington was located near a high school with a track. I jogged over daily to work out. Kyle drove to the school and met me, bringing my water bottle and workout equipment. He was a great coach and pushed me to work harder. When I thought I had no more energy, he encouraged me to pick up the pace. Kyle made a brave attempt to learn Shona and purchased a few books and videos to assist him. I was not a very good teacher, and consequently, he did not have the opportunity to practice Shona. We did not pursue it. I tried to be a good cook. We fell into a comfortable daily routine. However, the problem of getting a valid visa still loomed in the background, like a recurring nightmare.

I went online to the U.S. Citizenship and Naturalization Services webpage. A U.S. marriage-based green card would allow me to live and work in the country as a permanent resident. If I traveled abroad, I could return. The simplest way to get a green card was to have a resident family member as a sponsor. Up to this point in my life, I had no family members in the United States. I was on my

Chapter 20

own. When I married Kyle, he became my sponsor. Included in the application was a requirement to submit a certified marriage license, a copy of my Zimbabwe passport, Kyle's birth certificate as proof that Kyle was a U.S. citizen, and a utility bill with our names as proof of address. Fortunately, almost all of the answers to general questions could be completed online. I never consulted an immigration attorney because attorney fees were more than I could afford. Once everything was completed and submitted, I waited and waited. The "adjustment of status" process was taking a long time.

Chapter 21

In January 2010, I learned that my father had passed away peacefully lying in his bed. I could not believe it and was inconsolable. I called my siblings and talked with my mother. I desperately wanted to be with my family. My green card still had not been issued. I did not want to take the risk of traveling with my Zimbabwean passport. "Apply for an emergency travel document," my friend Sheila Lemuta said. "There is a special visa available in cases of death." I immediately requested and received an email with the official certificate of death from my father's doctor in Zimbabwe. After showing it to the Immigration Officer, to my surprise, I was immediately granted an emergency travel document. I quickly purchased a round-trip ticket. For two days I walked through airline terminals, got on and off planes, and waited anxiously between flights. It was agonizing. My niece, Chipo Munyaradzi, and her husband, Gidion, met me at the airport in Harare and drove me the long hours to get to my village. I did not make it home for the three days my father's body lay in our home, surrounded by family and mourners. I even missed my father's burial. I was told people came from far and wide to pay respects to the village chief. Kyle was supportive. We talked daily by phone. I cannot imagine making it through those agonizing weeks without him. It was good to see my mother and siblings, even under sad circumstances. I had been gone for six years. The homestead was deteriorating. My mother's bedroom had cracks and the roof was so rundown, a heavy rain might cause it to fall in. The walls of the kitchen were peeling. The economy of Zimbabwe was bad at the time, and everyone was suffering. The day after I arrived, I woke up early and visited my father's grave to pay my respects. I said a prayer kneeling next to his grave. I told him how much I missed him and was so sorry I couldn't come see him when he was sick. He knew I did not have a visa allowing me to visit. I had sent my father a new suit and he was proud of it. When he became ill, he told family members he wanted to be buried in it. Hearing his last words, I broke down into tears. I could tell my mother was devastated. She had lost weight. Yet she remained independent, going about her normal schedule. She cooked meals over an open fire in the kitchen

Chapter 21

house. She tended to her crop of maize, peanuts, and her vegetable garden. She washed clothes and hung them to dry. She cleaned the house and fed the chickens. Fortunately, Charles, my oldest brother, lived nearby. He and his family looked in on her and were available if she needed help. Everyone asked about my life in America. I showed them photos of my wedding and told them about Kyle. It was good to be with family and friends again. My heart ached when I left.

Chapter 22

In the spring of 2010, I looked around for an opportunity to return to the world of track. Not far from our home was Seattle Pacific University, a private liberal arts college. SPU competed in NCAA Division II. I contacted Erika Daligcon, head coach for the women's track program, and volunteered to help in any way I could. Erica invited me to come meet the team and allowed me to volunteer as an assistant distance running coach. Doris Brown Heritage, a famous distance runner, was also serving as a volunteer. From 1967 to 1971, Doris won the international cross-country title five times in a row for the United States. In 1999, she was the second female inducted into the United States Track Coaches Hall of Fame. Doris played a significant role in establishing the women's track program at Seattle Pacific University. I admired her. She was very supportive and gave me tips on how to be successful. "Have faith in yourself," she told me. "Listen to your body. It will tell you if something is not right." I remembered her advice every time I went for a run.

Erika Daligcon had been an SPU distance runner in both track and cross country. She took over the track program in 2008 and helped the SPU Falcons earn back-to-back fourth-place trophies at the NCAA Division II women's championships. Her women's squad won the Great Northwest Athletic Conference Championship. I was fortunate to be a part of the coaching team. The students asked me questions and seemed genuinely interested in the records I set in distance running. I enjoyed being back with a track program and an impressive one at that.

Every summer Seattle Pacific University sponsored a well-known Falcon running camp on Whidbey Island, in the northern boundary of Puget Sound. I volunteered to assist as a coach. We rode a ferry from Seattle to the island. I discovered beautiful forests and shaded running trails. Campers included middle and high school students who came for intensive training. Many athletes returned year after year and competed on a national level. Two workout sessions a day kept us focused, and in the evening we listened to inspirational speakers. I was asked to speak about my experience, my track achievements, and my commitment to distance

Chapter 22

running. "Running transformed my life," I told them. I was also asked to talk specifically about steeplechase drills because it was my specialty. A few students wanted me to suggest how they could improve their skills, especially in the cross-country races.

At the end of the summer, Coach Erica Daligcon left SPU on maternity leave, and I was employed to coach the cross-country track and field program until her return. I took on the head coaching role in distance running for both men and women. On the SPU Falcons website on August 19, 2010, I was quoted saying, "I'll be a little easy the first couple of weeks and make sure they're ready to start some real workouts." Coach Daligcon said, "We're really thrilled to have Letiwe on the coaching staff. She brings a lot of her expertise to this, as well as being very open to doing things in a slightly different way. And the fact that she already has a rapport with the returning athletes is going to make a big difference." A reporter for the *Seattle Times* asked about my style. "I'm pretty strict," I said. "I don't yell and bark, but when I say something, I mean it. I am very sensitive about showing up for practice on time. The athletes were a little bit laid back at the start, and I had to change everything around. Now, if practice starts at 9:30, they know if they come at 9:20, they are late. So they all show up at 9:15."

When I took the reins, the SPU Falcons website posted an article entitled, "A Long Way from Zimbabwe." The article read, "Letiwe Marakurwa Patton has displayed her running talents to the world as a member of the Zimbabwe national team. Ultimately, she would like to display them again in the 2012 Olympics." It was true. I did want to qualify for the Olympics in London and earn a spot on Zimbabwe's team. Coaching was a great opportunity for me to stay in shape. I wanted to defend my records. My personal best in the steeplechase was 9 minutes, 52.98 seconds, just four seconds off the provisional qualifying time of 9 minutes, 48 seconds. Coach Daligcon encouraged me. She said, "Letiwe still loves to run and is aiming at being competitive in the next few years. Part of effective coaching is knowing what the athlete is going through as far as race preparation, warm-up, and the psychological aspect." Coach Daligcon supported me and the students looked to me as the interim head coach. We got along. Sometimes they imitated my accent and we laughed. It didn't bother me. I felt confident taking on the challenge. Coach Daligcon wrote the workouts for each athlete, and I followed them. I adjusted the workout if there

Chapter 22

was an injury or illness and I increased workouts before an upcoming race. Coach Daligcon asked me if I would focus especially on coaching the athletes competing in the steeplechase. SPU did not have a standard-size track facility, but I set up hurdles on the track and had the runners jumping over and over. I put in extra time teaching them skills and techniques. At a conference competition, the SPU Falcon athletes scored well on the steeplechase. I was proud.

I accompanied the team traveling to cross-country meets at conference and regional races. Sometimes I was the only coach traveling with the team. We traveled as far away as Alaska. I made sure my athletes were physically prepared for the race. I wanted the students to improve their mental strength during the competition as well. I told them to "get in the zone and block stuff out." I remembered the inspiring talks Coach Wayne Phipps gave us before a meet and wanted to inspire my team with pep talks. I was grateful for the opportunity to coach a new generation of runners. The trip to Alaska was a first for me. We went in September during cross-country season, and it was already very cold. We flew to Anchorage, picked up a rental van, and I drove the team to Fairbanks, not far from the airport. I was a little nervous about driving to the hotel but soon noticed there were very few tall buildings and little traffic. The city almost looked deserted. It was beautiful and calm. The night before the track meet, the head coach of the University of Alaska in Fairbanks invited my team to a dinner with other athletes. It felt like a family get-together.

The teams geared up in bunnies, long-sleeved racing tops, long tights, and gloves. It was important to be adequately dressed for the weather conditions. We competed in several races. The women placed 2nd overall on the 6 km long course and placed 3rd overall as a team in the 4km short race. The men's team took 3rd place as a team. It was our season-opening competition, so we were able to see what we needed to work on. After the race, I drove the athletes back to the hotel to get changed and then took them out to eat. We walked around Fairbanks checking out the sights. The young people were happy with their performances and so was I. I couldn't wait to share the news with Erika and the rest of the athletic department. I felt a sense of accomplishment. When Coach Daligcon returned from maternity leave, she resumed her head coaching role and I continued to volunteer as an assistant. I inquired about possible coaching positions at SPU, but there were no openings for

Chapter 22

another full-time coach. It was time to look around for a salaried position.

Chapter 23

I received a letter from the U.S. Citizenship and Naturalization Service informing me that my status of adjustment was approved. I was elated! Before a green card could be issued, however, I was to provide a certified copy of my birth certificate, copies of previous work permits, and two new 2" x 2" photos. In addition, Immigration and Naturalization Services wanted proof my spouse could support me financially. I submitted our U.S. Federal income tax returns for the past three years and Kyle's earnings statement from his employer, Microsoft. Kyle paid the huge fee that accompanied the application. My fingerprints were taken, as they had been with every immigrant status application I had been required to submit, beginning with my first entry into the United States as an 18-year-old athlete. "I've had my fingerprints taken so many

Running to America

times," I joked, "I could never have lived a life of crime."

Within a few months, I received a very official-looking envelope. It was my green card, valid for two years! I showed it to Kyle. I told my family about it. With it came a welcoming letter and for the first time, I felt I was a part of a larger American family. Now I could travel in and out of the country without visa problems. I called my friends and shared the good news. A green card, however, did not grant citizenship. I could not vote or apply for a U.S. passport. Citizenship was further down the road, yet another goal. Immigrants who received a green card were given two years to qualify as a citizen before the card expired. I did not want to waste a second. I went on the U.S. Citizenship and Naturalization website and read the exhaustive list of requirements for a U.S. citizenship application. I smiled when I read the first item on the list. "Can you read, write, and speak English?" Yes! Check! I read further, "You will be tested on your knowledge of civics, primarily American history and U.S. government." I needed to know about the three branches of government and familiarize myself with the U.S. Constitution. I kept up with current events. I read practice questions and took practice tests online. Questions included, "What

Chapter 23

is the supreme law of the land? What do we call the first ten amendments to the Constitution? What did the Declaration of Independence do? Who becomes President if neither the President nor the Vice President can serve? What are two ways Americans can participate in their democracy? What is one reason colonists came to America? It would take time to prepare for the test, but I had two years to study. I resolved to take the test as soon as I felt ready.

Kyle and I had talked about traveling to Zimbabwe for over a year. I was now the proud holder of a green card. We could go! In December 2011, we packed our bags. Kyle's mother traveled with us. She was a world traveler and wanted to see and experience the culture in Zimbabwe as much as Kyle did. I was excited and a little anxious. Two cultures were about to collide, in a good way, I hoped. In Zimbabwe, family is everything. It defines who we are. I now had two families, one American and the other, African. Differences aside, both families were eager to meet.

Chapter 24

In the Harare airport in Zimbabwe, Kyle looked around. With few exceptions, he noted, everyone was black. He found the local people to be relaxed and friendly. We discovered some of our luggage did not make it, including Mother Patton's suitcase. It was bad news because she did not have a change of clothes. "Your luggage is in Ethiopia," I was told. "It will be put on the next plane to Harare." "Ethiopia?" I said. "What was it doing in Ethiopia?" We could not wait. I signed paperwork authorizing a relative in Harare to collect the luggage when it came. I was disappointed that our trip began with a frustrating experience.

My niece, Chipo Munyaradzi, and her husband, Gidion, graciously became our means of transportation. They drove us to a flea market where Mother Patton bought a few items of clothing before heading to the city of Gweru, about 277 km south, to spend the night with my sister, Emma, and her husband, Moses. My mother was waiting for me in Gweru, and as soon as we arrived, I ran into her arms. She was happy to meet Kyle, only seen in pictures up to this point. Although Mother Patton and my mother could not communicate verbally, their body language spoke for them. Both had big smiles.

When I planned our trip, I decided to begin with a visit to sites with upscale tourist accommodations. It would give Kyle and Mother Patton time to get acclimated before I introduced them to village life. We headed to Victoria Falls, the number one tourist site in the country. My mother joined us. It was the farthest she had ever traveled from her village, and I was excited for her. I had never been to the falls either. "The countryside looks very much like rural America with farmers working in the fields," said Mother Patton. She expected to see an abundance of wildlife and was surprised by the scarcity of wild animals. Kyle was concerned with the roads, littered with potholes and not well maintained. Speed limits were not enforced. As it turned dark, driving became even more hazardous. Cars approached us with only one headlight and many vehicles lacked taillights. Gidion drove carefully but other drivers were reckless, endangering everyone around them. When we arrived at the hotel in the town of Victoria Falls, we breathed

Chapter 24

a sigh of relief. It was a welcomed respite. It was my mother's first stay in a hotel and a nice one at that. She was awed by the soft beds, the nice clean sheets, and the bathrooms with running water, a lifestyle she considered luxurious.

Victoria Falls sits on the border of Zambia and Zimbabwe and is known as "the world's greatest sheet of falling water," and "one of the world's largest waterfalls." It was awesome, a powerful force of nature. We went on a sunset cruise on the Zambezi River and saw hippos, giraffes, monkeys, baboons, and warthogs—animals once wild and abundant, now found only at wildlife preserves. Mother Patton was delighted. At lookout points, we felt the mist and spray as water thundered down drowning out all other sounds. I was pleased that Kyle, Mother Patton, and my mother were enjoying themselves. I prided myself on selecting a popular site to visit. Victoria Falls was a good idea. With renewed energy, we headed back to Gweru.

"Our luggage!" we cried out, as we entered Emma's house. Our wayward suitcases were lined up awaiting our arrival. We were thrilled. This was made possible because a thoughtful relative collected the luggage from the Harare airport, drove all the way to Gweru, deposited our luggage, and then drove back home. It was a wonderful gift, and just in time for Christmas. On Christmas Day, at least twenty-five relatives came to visit. Christmas in Zimbabwe does not include presents, but I wanted to give something from America to family members. One of my suitcases was filled with gifts. I gave soccer jerseys to the men, and they were pleased. I gave clothing to the women, and they were delighted. I guessed their sizes and found I had guessed correctly. It brought me such happiness. Kyle found everyone to be appreciative of the gifts although they had not expected it. Coming together as a family was the best gift. We talked and talked, and I caught up on the news. It was a great homecoming.

Chapter 25

After Christmas, we headed toward South Africa, a country that borders Zimbabwe to the south. Chipo and Gidion were once again our drivers. My mother did not have a passport and could not come with us. She returned to her village to wait for our arrival a week later. Kyle and Mother Patton produced American passports at the border. They were told to enjoy their stay. I traveled with my Zimbabwean passport along with Chipo and Gidion. We were asked a lot of questions. Why were we visiting South Africa? Who were we visiting? How long would we stay? Zimbabwean citizens migrate to South Africa for various reasons, including economic opportunities and a search for better living conditions. The border guards finally seemed satisfied with our answers and we were allowed to enter. A woman at the border crossing caught Kyle's eye. She was carrying a baby on her back, breastfeeding another baby, and carrying a big bucket on her head. He thought it was amazing. It was interesting for me to see my culture through his eyes. Such sights are not familiar to Westerners.

A friend invited us to stay at his home in Johannesburg for the night. It was in a quiet neighborhood, and we were grateful for a good night's rest. The next day we journeyed south to Durban, a modern city on the Indian Ocean. Zimbabwe is a landlocked country, and I thought the ocean scenery of South Africa would be relaxing. The roads in South Africa were much improved over Zimbabwe. The surrounding countryside was beautifully landscaped. Our Airbnb on the ocean was just as I had pictured it. We walked on the beach and were drenched by waves. We visited Ushaka Marine World and shopped at a mall. It was not much different from an American beach resort.

At the border with Zimbabwe, we joined a long line of cars and people. Traffic was moving slowly, and it was hot. January in Zimbabwe is like summer in America. The seasons are reversed. Every car was searched for contraband. I had stopped to buy groceries to take to the homestead and even the food was searched. We were finally cleared to go. Thankfully, Gidion had relatives across the border, and we stopped for the night. It had been a long day, and his family was welcoming. I lay in bed thinking about the next day. What would be Kyle's

Chapter 25

reaction when he saw my village, my childhood home, my people? I did not know if I had prepared him. How do you prepare a westerner for a rural village in Zimbabwe? Would he get sick drinking the water? Would he be sensitive to the sights and smells of farm animals and outhouses? How would the villagers see my husband and mother-in-law? Would they be accepted? I did not know what to expect or how we would be received.

I should not have worried. Our arrival was turned into a homecoming and a celebration. I was never so proud of my village as I was that day. Amidst singing and clapping we were met and ushered into my mother's large round kitchen house, where men and women sat on opposite sides of the room. Emma's husband Moses gave greetings in both English and Shona so everyone could understand. He showed Kyle a traditional greeting given by men in my culture by clapping hands, with fingers, thumbs, and palms aligned. Women clapped their palms together with their hands at a right angle. After we properly greeted everyone, the women sang traditional songs and danced. A nephew arranged to have our church youth choir come and sing. I had not expected a large and jubilant turnout. Kyle and Mother Patton were treated as honored guests, almost like royalty. As a daughter of the tribe, I had journeyed far away and returned. For the first time, I brought my American family home. It was a special moment for both sides.

As I expected, life in my homestead was a bit of a rough experience for Kyle and Mother Patton. They were learning to do without some of the comforts of home. There was no running water in the house. Drinking and cooking water was brought from the well. In the outhouse, the toilet did not flush. I introduced Kyle to the way locals take showers. I gave him a bucket filled with warm water and showed him an enclosed structure attached to the outhouse where he could bathe. I was grateful for his efforts to fit in. Mother Patton was experienced in adapting to other cultures. Kyle's father had a long career in the U.S. Navy, and the family had lived overseas. She adjusted as she always had. Because we were honored guests, Kyle and I were given a room with a bed, as was Mother Patton. The rest of the women slept on mats or blankets on the floor in the living room and in the kitchen house. The men piled into a spare room and Charles's house next door. Other men brought tents and slept outside.

Kyle noticed that many of the villagers were poor and worked hard but did not seem worried or

Chapter 25

stressed. The days passed in a relaxed manner. Men and women were generally segregated by choice. As a result, Kyle spent most of his time with my brothers. They spoke English and engaged Kyle in conversation. One afternoon as they sat drinking beer, I heard Kyle share his impression of a bungee jumper at Victoria Falls. An animated discussion followed. "Why," they said, "would anyone want to put their lives in such danger?" They talked and laughed easily as if they had known each other for years. I relaxed. Things were going well.

Kyle watched a woman braiding my hair. It took her about twenty minutes. She then braided my sister's hair, and a few minutes later, quickly braided the hair of two more women. He said, "If she worked braiding hair in America, with her skill and speed, she could make a fortune." Mother Patton came from New Orleans, home of Cajun and Creole food. She found the local food a little bland but graciously ate it without comment. I was glad I had brought groceries so our meals could be varied. Before the trip, Mother Patton's hair was professionally curled. It looked nice throughout the journey. A few women in the village were curious about her curly hair, prompting them to want to verify whether it was real or a hairpiece. Mother Patton allowed them to feel it. They laughed. It was a great icebreaker. I planned for us to stay in my village for only a few days. It was long enough for a first visit. Two cultures had come together with me in the center. Rather than colliding, as I had feared, both cultures were enhanced, and my heart overflowed with joy.

Back in Harare, we spent the night at the home of my nephew's friend, in a well-secured and gated neighborhood. At the airport, I thanked Gidion and Chipo for transporting us across two countries! Without them, the journey would not have occurred. We were privileged to have an amazing network of hospitality. For weeks we were lovingly passed from relative to relative, from friend to friend, from home to home, and welcomed warmly at each stop along the way. Family truly was everything.

Chapter 26

In January 2012, I applied for the position of head coach at Eastside Catholic High School. The school was in Sammamish, Washington on land historically belonging to the Coast Salish Indigenous People. It was about a 30-minute drive from where we lived. After my interview, I was offered the position and accepted. The high school students reminded me of the kids at the summer camp. Racing events were in the Seattle area, and I soon became familiar with parts of the city I had not explored. I did not feel comfortable driving the school bus, and to my relief, another employee in the school drove us to and from the track meets. I recruited two assistant coaches, ordered new uniforms, and began organizing the track program. The boys and girls were well-behaved, and it made my job enjoyable. One boy was so good at running long distances that he was consistently one of the top three winners at each race. Other kids did not perform as well but they always did their best and I cheered them on, supporting their efforts regardless of performance. I built a good relationship with parents who came out to support the team. They organized dinners and planned the end of season celebration.

I was fortunate to be healthy up to this point in my track career. But it did not last. I began having problems with my knee. I nursed it for a while, easing up on workouts. When it did not improve, I consulted a physician. An MRI did not show any injury, so I continued my workouts. Then my ankle became swollen and ached. I wrapped it to ease the pain. Eventually, it healed but I missed out on weeks of training. I eased back into running and planned to enter several meets. It did not happen. I developed pain in my left hamstring. I could not run or put pressure on my left leg. A physical therapist recommended I have an MRI of my back. That was surprising because my back was not in pain. However, the MRI showed a bulging disc on my lower back causing my hamstring to hurt. I received a painful injection. I took time off to heal and to allow medication to work. I decided to compete in the steeplechase at the Oregon Invitation. My time was two minutes more than my record. It was disappointing. The idea of hanging up my spikes and ending my career began to enter

Chapter 26

my thoughts. Perhaps my body was ready for me to take a different direction.

Kyle and I always planned to have children and now it seemed to be the right time. As if on cue, we discovered that we were going to have a baby girl. Along with the exciting news of my pregnancy came a coaching opportunity at San Jose State University in San Jose, California. I learned about the assistant cross-country coach position from the university head coach. The position came with a one-year commitment. I applied and was hired. Kyle and I had talked about moving to California and now we had the opportunity. We moved to San Jose, and I began working in August. The coaching went well. I continued working throughout my pregnancy. When Caryn was born, I realized my world had significantly changed. I was breastfeeding Caryn, so I pumped a lot of milk each day. I was constantly exhausted and struggled with it, but when I looked at my daughter's face, it was worth it. She was healthy and doing well. Kyle commuted to work but when he arrived home, he did nothing but hold his baby. We enjoyed being parents, although we were constantly tired. At the end of the year, the head coach was let go and San Jose State University also terminated all the assistant coaching positions. I regretted dragging

Kyle to San Jose with only a one-year contract. It was a risk but did not go in our favor. It was at this point that I decided it was time to leave coaching and look for other career opportunities.

Chapter 27

I focused on studying for the citizenship civics test by studying material provided on the U.S. Citizenship and Immigration Services website. American friends told me I knew more about civics than they did. In 2013, I scheduled an appointment for a required in-person test to be conducted by an Immigration and Naturalization Services Officer. The day arrived and I went to my appointment at the scheduled time. This was it. I was going to pass or fail. I looked around at people waiting nervously. Had I learned enough? I knew I had to get six out of ten questions correct, but there were a hundred questions he could ask. I heard my name called and walked toward the office with my heart beating rapidly. I was sweating. I shook hands with the officer, entered the room, and took a seat.

The officer was a middle-aged man with a pleasant smile. I knew his job was to interview me and test my knowledge of civics. He opened my file, confirmed who I was, and began asking civics questions. I knew the answers and responded quickly. After a few questions and answers, he looked at the file again. "You have been in the country since you were eighteen years old," he said. "Why did you come to America?" "I was on an Olympics Solidarity Scholarship in track," I responded. "Tell me about your experience," he said. I talked. I had not expected to be asked about being an athlete. I hoped I was not rambling. He seemed interested and I relaxed. He made notations in the file. "You attended high school, college, and graduate school in America." "Yes," I said. "I see you are from Zimbabwe," he noted. "Yes," I said. He made more notations in the file and said, "I recently traveled to Zimbabwe with my family and enjoyed visiting the country." He seemed genuinely interested in my homeland, and we chatted about Zimbabwe and the places he had visited. Then he closed the file. I had been in his office for less than ten minutes. He looked at me and said, "You have passed the citizenship test. Congratulations." He shook my hand. A wide smile spread across my face. I knew my interview had gone well. I was lucky. No, not lucky, I thought. I was blessed. My smile changed to tears as I walked to my car. How long had I worked and prayed for this moment? I was finally going to become a citizen of the United

Chapter 27

States! I had to tell Kyle. It was time to celebrate. I would be notified of the day to take the official oath in a ceremony.

I could not imagine the variety of interviews USCIS Officers conduct daily with immigrants. Statistically, about 88% pass, and of those who do not pass, 7% pass the second time. The few who do not pass the test probably do not speak or read English well enough to communicate or have not studied properly for the civics exam. Many never make it to an interview because their applications are incorrect or incomplete or they cannot manage to obtain the required documentation. Some immigrants cannot pay the fees required. A few try to hide arrest records, are in arrears on child support, or have failed to pay debts. Some simply do not try to obtain citizenship and seek other ways to remain in the country. It is an overwhelming process. Those who complete the citizenship test are welcomed into this great country of immigrants. It had been my dream to be one of them.

Within a month I was provided the date and place of the official oath ceremony. When the day for my naturalization came, I was accompanied by Kyle, my baby daughter Caryn, and Mother Patton. I was required to relinquish my permanent resident card—my green card. We entered

Running to America

a large room filled with immigrants and their families. I found my assigned seat. A judge walked out and stood before us. We were asked to stand and pledge allegiance to the flag of the United States. The judge told us there were many ways to serve as good citizens, to serve on juries when called, to participate in democracy, and to abide by the laws. Then came the big moment. There is nothing to equate the experience of standing with people from every country on earth, raising hands in unison and declaring on oath, to support and defend the Constitution and laws of the United States of America against all enemies, foreign and domestic, and to bear true faith and allegiance to the same. After the oath, we fell silent. Then we cheered. We clapped. We cried. It was emotional. We congratulated each other. I was handed an envelope with my naturalization certificate and told to keep it in a safe place. We were given small American flags. Caryn took possession of my flag and would not let go. I was glad she was present on this momentous day. She would grow up as an American citizen. As part of her heritage, she would also grow up knowing her Zimbabwean family. I would make sure of that. It was a promise I made to myself and to her. Kyle and Caryn accompanied me to a scheduled appointment at the

Chapter 27

US Post Office to formally apply for my passport. I showed my naturalization certificate. It was a simple procedure. Kyle also applied for a passport, and I completed one for Caryn. We were required to submit a birth certificate for Caryn confirming we were her parents. It was a great day when our passports came in the mail.

In 2014 we bought a house in San Francisco. I decided to travel to Zimbabwe for the first time using my American passport. Because Caryn was under age two, she could fly for free on international flights. I was not sure how she would react to flying. Apparently, she liked it because she slept for much of the trip. It allowed me to sleep as well. Kyle did not accompany us. The trip was primarily to visit my mother and let her hold her grandbaby. When we arrived, she put Caryn on her back, securing her with a long cloth wound around both of them, as is the custom in Zimbabwe. Caryn rode happily attached to my mother, her *gogo*, as she worked on her farm. Sometimes my mother sang nursery songs in Shona to put Caryn to sleep. Caryn had been eating solid food, and she took easily to eating sadza. When my cousins came to visit with their children, Caryn played happily and performed a few antics making us all laugh. She adjusted to the rhythms of village life and did not get sick. She and my mother became inseparable. My mother told me that Caryn looked like me when I was a child. I would never know because there are no pictures of my childhood.

Chapter 28

I entered a few local track meets in the San Francisco area, but working and caring for Caryn was a full-time job. I discovered I was going to have child number two! Alexander came into our lives and our household became much busier. I worked in downtown San Francisco in guest services for a big hotel and enjoyed my job. One day I came home from work and found Mama Becky walking around holding Alexander. Mama Becky and Dan visited us for a few days, and we took them to see the sights with babies in tow. Seeing Mama Becky holding Alexander reminded me of how much I missed my mother, and I knew she missed seeing her grandchildren. She had not met Alexander. Although I talked with her by phone frequently, it was not the same as being with her. However, life with two babies demanded most of my time, and traveling with them around the world was out of the question. I decided to work on getting my mother a travel visa so she could come visit us. It would be easier for me if she could come to America than it would be for me to travel to Zimbabwe with two little ones. She was denied a visitor's visa three times.

As a U.S. citizen, I learned I could submit a Form I-130, Petition for Alien Relative. It was the first step of a process allowing my mother to apply to immigrate to the United States and get a green card, a permanent resident card. Since a travel visa was not working, why not jump right into sponsoring her for a green card? I applied to the U.S. Citizenship and Immigration Services along with copies of our birth certificates showing we were mother and daughter. The application was approved. My mother was told to get clearance from officials in Zimbabwe. She was required to get a physical examination from an approved immigration physician. We waited for the petition to be approved. It was! The next step was to submit a form for her to become a legal permanent resident of the United States. Once she arrived in the U.S., I planned to apply for her to get a green card. I had learned a lot in obtaining my own green card. I could not believe how fast the process was moving for my mother.

The day came for my mother to arrive in San Francisco. It was a mind-blowing experience. At

Chapter 28

age 78 she left Zimbabwe for the first time, by herself. She had rarely traveled from her village and had never been on an airplane. She knew no English and had no idea how long the trip would take. She only knew that the airplane would fly to America, to me. I worried that perhaps I had made a mistake having her travel alone. What if she got lost? What if she got sick? How would I find her? She had no cell phone. I completed paperwork requesting that flight attendants meet her at each landing and transport her by wheelchair to her next flight and to the baggage claim area where I would meet her. The travel took a heavy toll. When she landed in San Francisco, she was exhausted and somewhat disoriented. When I saw her, it was a beautiful sight and a tremendous relief. My heart swelled with joy. She suddenly recognized me and knew she had arrived. We hugged and hugged.

I was eager to tell her about my life and show her the city and Bay area. San Francisco must have looked so strange to her. I hoped she would settle in once we arrived home. Caryn and Alexander were excited about seeing their *gogo*. It did not matter that she knew no English. I gave her a chance to rest and get used to the new time zone. She went for a walk every day up and down the hilly streets by herself. She was constantly amazed at everything she saw. She cooked us Zimbabwean meals but was very uncomfortable cooking on a gas stove. I knew there was no way we were going to build a fire in the backyard for cooking. She understood. She discovered American hot dogs and loved eating them. At the mall, she found a place that cooked chicken to her liking and we went there often. She said that visiting America was the best gift anyone had ever given her.

I applied for my mother to get a green card and it came in the mail. The green card was good for 10 years, but conditions came with the card. If she were to leave the U.S., she would have to return within 6 months. If she stayed out of the U.S. for longer than 12 months, she was required to submit a form for the "Returning Resident Visa." As time went by, I realized my mother missed her home, her farm, her other children, and their families, and so the time came for her to go. She stayed with us from September 2016 through January 2017, and I loved every minute. I decided to visit her more often.

After a year I booked flights to Zimbabwe. This time I was taking Alexander, who was still under two years of age and could fly for free on international flights. I left Caryn home and in good hands with Kyle and Mother Patton. I would not be gone

Chapter 28

long. Alexander was as good a traveler as Caryn had been. We arrived in April and the weather was nice. Alexander was full of energy and immediately began running around playing with his cousins. He loved chasing chickens and kicking a ball around the front yard. My mother loved seeing her grandson again and he remembered her. She wrapped him up on her back, walked, and sang to him until he fell asleep. Although he did not speak any Shona, he seemed to understand what was said to him. One day I noticed he had a rash. It soon spread all over his body. I rushed him to the nearest clinic where he was given an injection. I did not know what caused it. Could it have been something he ate or drank or an allergic reaction? The rash itched and irritated him. The injection helped and finally, the rash went away. I was greatly relieved.

I was still breastfeeding Alexander who was eighteen months old. "You must stop breastfeeding him," my mother said. "He is too old for it. You must wean him." When I tried to stop, he cried continuously. "Let me take him to sleep in my room tonight," my mother said. I agreed. I did not know if it was a good idea and fully expected he would cry all night. But he didn't. He slept all night without being breastfed and without being with me. However, during the day he would come to me and cry wanting to be breastfed. It was painful. "Maybe I should wait until I get home," I said. But my mother encouraged me to be patient. She kept Alexander at night in her room and he continued sleeping through the night without crying for milk. On the flight home, he did not cry for milk at all. I felt a major sense of accomplishment even though it was my mother's guidance that enabled me to get Alexander through this developmental stage. I missed not having my mother around to share the joys and frustrations of raising children and looked forward to her next visit.

Fortunately, my mother was able to visit us again several times. She was in her eighties but in good health. We arranged for my nephew, Itayi Mutandi, to accompany her to the airport in Harare and meet her upon her return. With Itayi nearby, my mother always confidently boarded the airplane, assured it was the correct one. Once, however, after disembarking on a leg of a trip from San Francisco to Zimbabwe, my mother refused to board the airplane because Itayi was not in the boarding area. She forgot that she had one more flight before arriving home. The boarding process came to a halt. A flight attendant looked at my mother's passport to determine her citizenship. She noted my mother was from Zimbabwe and

Chapter 28

guessed she was speaking Shona. She called Tafara, a friend from Zimbabwe who was told about the problem and agreed to speak with my mother by phone. In Shona, Tafara said, "Don't worry. Itayi knows about this flight, and it is the correct one. You must get on. He will be waiting for you when you get off in Harare." Only then did my mother board the airplane. I was thankful for Tafara and the flight attendant who delayed boarding a few extra minutes to comfort and reassure an old woman.

Chapter 29

In 2021 we bought a vacation house in Palm Springs, California. On our honeymoon driving tour, we had driven through Palm Springs and decided we would move to the area if an opportunity arose. We looked forward to opportunities to visit the area. Then covid-19 hit the nation and Kyle was able to work remotely. Suddenly we were not tied to San Francisco and could move anywhere we chose. It did not take us long to decide where we wanted to go. In 2022 we sold our house in San Francisco and moved. Palm Springs became our residence. I did not miss the rain, the fog, and the chilly climate. I loved the desert air. I began homeschooling and discovered educational software programs allowing the kids to progress at their own rate. We connected with other homeschooled families in the area. The children participated in local children's theater and junior pilot programs.

In December 2022, Kyle and I traveled to Zimbabwe with the kids, ages seven and ten. We planned to arrive at my mother's homestead on Christmas Eve. First, however, we wanted to see a few natural wonders in the country. We spent the first night at Itayi's home. The next day, the four of us piled in his van. We squeezed in a few more family members and were off on an adventure. Itayi drove us to the Mtarazi Falls National Park in the Eastern Highlands. Most tourists visit the well-known Victoria Falls. Few ever go to the remote Mtarazi Falls. Accessible from Mutare, the park is a rough 4-hour drive on a dusty unpaved road littered with rocks and full of holes. Itayi maneuvered around the debris and hoped the van would not break down. The road slowly increased in elevation. A nice hotel sat at the top of the mountain. Tourists were out and about. Walking trails led to views of mountain ranges and the falls. We saw a chasm overlooking a waterfall plunging 2500 feet below into the Honde Valley. Over the chasm was a narrow suspension bridge. Those who were brave could walk across the skywalk. For the super brave, there was a zipline, and for the suicidal, a bungy jump. We planned to walk across the skywalk.

We saw a few people carefully walking out on the skywalk. It was too dangerous for the kids. We left them at an overlook with Itayi and other family members so they could watch. Kyle and

Chapter 29

I got in line. A park employee strapped us into harnesses with a wire clipped to the bridge railing. Suddenly it was our turn. Kyle and I grabbed the railing and slowly stepped onto the skywalk, constructed of wood planks with wire handrails. A guide accompanied us. The bridge swayed slightly, and I held on tighter. Maybe this was not a good idea. Although I was surrounded by 360° views of natural landscapes and beautiful mountain ranges, I focused solely on maintaining my balance. As I reached the middle of the skywalk, I finally stopped and looked around. At eye level, a waterfall poured down the chasm. I could feel the spray against my skin. What an amazing view! We made it across and back. It was exhilarating. On our drive back, the van got stuck in the mud. Through God's grace and with the help of a good Samaritan family, we pushed and rocked the van and finally, it cleared the mud and rolled onto a flat surface.

I told my niece, Beula, and sister, Jenipher, about our planned arrival home on December 24th, but I did not tell my mother. I did not want her to worry. A few of my siblings and their families were visiting at the homestead for the Christmas holiday. We arrived in Itayi's van, and I ran over to give my mother a big hug. At 85 she looked healthy and fit. She was a little disoriented when she saw us but quickly realized who we were. As always, she gathered us in her living room for a thanksgiving prayer. We sang and thanked God for a safe arrival. We continued talking until everyone fell asleep.

I slept in my mother's room with my sisters. We spread out on the bed and over the floor on blankets and mats. My sister Tabeth was the most talkative. She began telling a story about me. It took place when I was very young. My mother took me along to run an errand. A bus came and my mother began to board. She thought I was with her, but never having seen a bus before, I was scared and ran away. My mother ran after me, and I ran faster. My mother chased me, embarrassed in front of the people watching. Tabeth acted out my mother yelling and chasing after me. As my sister told the story, we laughed until our lungs hurt. It was the best time I've ever had with my sisters.

On Christmas Day the kids were up with the chickens. Literally. Alexander was gingerly picking up a chicken after chasing it around the dirt yard. He proudly held up the multi-colored bird. Then Caryn picked up a chicken. I hoped they would not get pecked. In the yard I began stirring a big pot of scrambled eggs over a fire to go with hot tea and bread. I offered on many occasions to buy my mother an electric or gas stove, but she preferred

Chapter 29

to cook over a fire. My sisters and I cooked special treats for the holiday including sadza, lamb, goat meat and relish. As we ate our Christmas dinner, I looked around at my big extended family and my heart filled with joy.

Over the next few days as my siblings left to go home, we settled in. The children and their new friends ran around. The kids loved being outdoors and did not miss television or their electronic devices. At night I gazed at the stars, so clear and bright in the night sky that they lit up the village. When it rained, Alexander drew a picture of the kitchen round house in the mud. It included windows and a doorstep. What better material for creating a work of art than mud? Over the years I was able to send my mother money to build a permanent roof for the kitchen structure. It was well built and sturdy and she was very happy. The homestead was also improved. I felt much better about my mother's living conditions.

Certain aspects of village life took a while to get used to. The homestead still had no running water. The bathroom toilet did have a chamber to sit on. Beside it was a bucket of water which took the place of flushing. Every day my niece and aunt who cared for my mom, walked about half a mile to fetch clean water at the well and carry it back on their heads. Caryn wanted to try it, so we found her a medium size plastic container. I was impressed with her ability to carry the container with water on her head all the way back to the house without dropping it. She was very proud. Kyle rolled a wheelbarrow to the well with two containers. He filled them with water and pushed the wheelbarrow back to the house. It was a warm day, and he was dripping with sweat. I was proud of the effort my family made to experience village life. With some of the water Kyle brought from the well, I began washing clothes. I filled one bucket with water and soap suds for washing clothes and another bucket for rinsing. I scrubbed and rinsed our clothes and hung them up to dry. My back and arms were sore. It was another reminder of my former life. I missed my washer and dryer. My oldest sister, Emma, was not able to visit with us at my mother's house so we drove to her house in the city of Gweru. City life was somewhat different from village life but had its own problems. Emma said there were talks of cutting electricity for part of the day. The city was also experiencing a water shortage. We celebrated New Year's Day eating and enjoying our time together.

Chapter 30

Itayi, who was beginning to tire from driving us around, took us for a final sightseeing drive in Harare before taking Kyle to the airport to travel home for work commitments. The children and I planned to stay a few more weeks. We drove through Borrowdale, an affluent and prestigious residential and shopping suburb. I had never seen this neighborhood. The huge lawns, gardens, and parks were carefully manicured. Built originally as a white enclave, both white and black families now lived in the upscale community. The late President Robert Mugabe once lived in Borrowdale. It was quiet, a different feel from the pedestrian crowds in downtown Harare. We gave Kyle a good send-off at the airport and spent the night at Itayi's house in Marondera. Itayi was incredible and without him, I doubt we could or would have made the trip.

Back at the homestead, I volunteered to clean and cook. I purchased two goats, lots of chickens, bread, and a few crates of drinks. We ate fresh vegetables from the garden. The food was healthy and organic. My brothers oversaw the killing of animals and the cutting of meat in preparation for cooking. A few days later, I grabbed my cell phone to call Kyle. I could not connect to the local network. After numerous failed attempts, my sister let me use her phone and I got through. It was comforting to talk with him. After the call, I put away my phone and did not try to use it again. If I could not get on the local network, it was useless. I slipped out of the house for a walk. I wanted to breathe deeply of the place where my life began.

Schools in Zimbabwe opened and my kids were excited when I told them they could go to school for a day or two. I took them to the same primary school I attended as a child, the Hande Primary School. The headmaster and some of the teachers remembered me from having attended the school and the children gathered around me. They were excited to see this former student. The schoolchildren claimed the two newcomers as friends right away. After classes began I walked around the school and peeked into classrooms. The kids were squeezed together with two or three students to a desk. Each room was overflowing with children. Supplies were low. Some students did not even have pencils. The school headmaster hoped to get

Chapter 30

donations so more desks could be bought. The teachers were gracious in allowing my children to visit and they had a wonderful time. Itayi returned and took us to his home in Marondera. He wanted the kids to experience Rapids Academy, a private school where he is the director. It is one of the top schools in the Marondera District. Itayi provided uniforms for both kids and they loved being around other children. The buildings were new and the ratio of teacher to student was much lower than in my village school.

Driving on secondary and rural roads in Zimbabwe remained perilous over the years. Large numbers of accidents occured every day. Most injuries were the result of speeding and not wearing seat belts. One day when I was in the village, local children climbed into their school bus as usual. A short time later, the bus was involved in a terrible accident. Everyone rushed to the hospital. We learned two of the children and a young man on the bus died. Many were critically injured. I heard wailing in the halls of the hospital and many families in the village were grieving. My mother was devastated. She knew a young man on the bus who died. He had often stopped by to check on her. It was painful to see my mother grieve. I went to the homes of the deceased to show respect. The women were crying, and the men were suffering from within, not expressing grief outwardly. Village women started a fire outside and fetched water. They began cooking to feed the people coming to the funeral. The young man who died was a member of my church, and the congregation came to lay him to rest. His father was so emotional he could not speak at the funeral, so my brother Darlington spoke for him. Songs were sung. Scriptures read. The pastor said a few words and blessed the body as it was lowered into the grave.

After a few more days it was time to return home. We gathered for prayer and squeezed as many family members as we could into the car for the drive to the airport. After many hugs, the kids and I headed through the terminal. At passport control I was told we overstayed our 30-day visa and owed a penalty payment of $300.00. I argued with the passport control officer because in December, upon entry in Harare, I paid the fee for the privilege of staying longer than 30 days. We argued some more and finally he agreed I could pay $30.00 per person if we did not re-enter Zimbabwe within a certain time frame. It was confusing and frustrating. Who was I going to complain to? The system was what it was. We went through security and barely made our flight to Durban, South Africa. When we arrived,

Chapter 30

my niece Chipo and her son met us and drove us to their home for a few days of relaxation before the long trip back. I needed the time to decompress. The weather was nice, so the kids and I sat on a covered porch as school lessons continued. I insisted they spend part of each day focused on math and reading assignments. I wondered if they were aware of the difference between my village school and the educational opportunities they had in America. I suspect their visit to the Hande Primary School would only be remembered as a fun day with new friends. Perhaps it should be.

Chapter 31

When I stayed in the Savannah International Training Center, I not only made friends but found a second family. We shared much more than a building. We built relationships and countless memories. However, when the center closed, we all went our separate ways. We scattered to places across the country and around the world.

An idea began to take shape in my mind—a reunion in Savannah, Georgia, the place where we shared so many memories. Despite my initial doubts about the feasibility of gathering everyone together after twenty-three years, I decided to give it a shot. I created a WhatsApp group with a few athletes I had stayed in touch with over the years. Through this group, I asked members to help spread the word. The response was overwhelmingly positive, and everyone thought a reunion was a fantastic idea. The planning phase, however, proved to be more challenging than anticipated. Yet, despite the difficulties, I remained committed to making it happen. As more athletes joined the chat group, I suggested that we make it a Friday-Sunday event in the summer of 2023. Everyone agreed.

With the dates set, the planning process began in earnest. I sent numerous messages and ideas to the group. Thankfully, a few individuals like George Maringapasi, Ruth Mansogo, Ousman Diarra, Abderaman Brahim, and Eric N'dri stepped forward with their thoughts and suggestions. I continued sending out ideas and recommendations for the reunion.

During the planning phase, Ousman delivered wonderful news—he had arranged for one of the host couples, Spencer and Terri Wheeler, to open the grounds of their beautiful home in Vernonburg, just outside Savannah, for the reunion. The house was situated on the Vernon River on a beautiful tract of land with breathtaking views. The Wheelers' generosity in providing food, drinks, and entertainment, and in opening their doors to our large group was an incredible gift.

Excitedly, I created an Evite to share all the details of the reunion, and it was heartwarming to see the responses. I purchased airline tickets for my family to travel to Savannah for the reunion. Time could not pass fast enough as I eagerly waited to see my friends again. We arrived in Savannah

Chapter 31

a week before the reunion and stayed with Mama Becky. On Sunday we attended the service at the First Presbyterian Church of Savannah, the church I attended when I lived at the center. Accompanied by Pastor Stephen Williams, John and Ann Tatum, and Mama Becky, we went to eat after the service and talked for hours. I visited my host father, Arthur Peagler, my dear country friend, Tina Papaya, and other host families I stayed in touch with for so many years. We drove by Jenkins High School, and I was amazed at the beautiful new buildings and campus.

Ruth Mansogo found a restaurant that could accommodate all 24 of us on Friday night. Sitting together at a long table, we enjoyed a fantastic meal and reflected on our good fortune to reunite after so many years. Brahim and his wife, Talia, graciously hosted the athletes for breakfast at their home on Saturday morning. Before heading to the BBQ party that evening, we athletes gathered for a group photo at the former Savannah International Training Center, now known as Cohen's Retreat, an upscale restaurant and specialty shop hub.

All the host families and friends joined the reunion on Saturday. It was a magnificent celebration and filled my heart with joy. Everyone shared the same sentiment. I was thrilled to introduce my family to my former teammates and equally excited to meet their families. Tina Paulino traveled all the way from Italy to be there. Others journeyed from locations around the United States. Our former coach, Abdi Bile, and his wife traveled from Minnesota to join us, a truly special moment. We had once been young athletes under his responsibility and his guidance was invaluable. He watched us interact, excited as children at a party.

I believe family includes those we choose to have in our lives. I consider the athletes I trained with in Savannah to be part of my extended family. We continue to support and uplift each other. The reunion was a testament to the enduring power of friendship and the impact that shared passions have on our lives. Running, whether for competition or for sheer enjoyment, has always held tremendous significance for me, and it continues to shape my life in many ways. It gives me a sense of purpose. I will always be forever grateful for the talent that God has given me. In running I find joy and peace. I would never trade it for anything. The lives of my children will be very different from mine. They will not know my story unless I tell it. Perhaps they are the reason I wrote this memoir. For them. For Kyle. For everyone who may enjoy reading about

Chapter 31

my homeland, my journey to America, and my joy in running.

Acknowledgements

I would like to thank the members of my family who contributed to this memoir. I thank my husband Kyle, who read a draft of the text and recalled memories of our journey together and Kyle's mother, Hildegarde Lewis Patton for her recollections. My mother, Siwisa Marakurwa, and my siblings were great contributors. I thank Tina Papaya, a fellow Zimbabwean, who read a draft and shared comments. I am blessed with many friends and colleagues who allowed me to engage them in recalling details of our past.

I am grateful to the people of my village who shaped my life and celebrated the visits of my American family. I thank Itayi Mutandi and Gidion and Chipo Munyaradzi for their hospitality and transportation in Zimbabwe. Rapids Academy and Hande Primary School were gracious in allowing my children to attend classes for a few days during our visit.

I thank my editor and friend, Rebecca Rowden, without whom this memoir would never have taken shape. I refer to her in the book as "Mama Becky." When I began the hard work of writing this memoir, she constantly engaged me in dialogue, encouraged me to recall details, both good and bad, asked me to confirm facts and to reach out to family and friends. She took my long rambling drafts and crafted them into a readable memoir. I am grateful for her guidance and friendship.

I am grateful for the talent of Bana Balleh who created and designed the front cover of my book. Bana is a graduate of the Savannah College of Art and Design, and her creative artwork can be seen on her web page www.banaballeh.com.

About the Author

Letiwe Marakurwa Patton

As a young girl living in Zimbabwe, the author discovered she had a talent—running. She joined a local track club, was mentored by a dedicated coach, and eagerly entered the world of cross-country track competition. Her meteoric rise was a surprise, but it was not without sacrifice. She became the Junior Women's World Cross-Country Champion of Zimbabwe. At the age of eighteen, with the goal of becoming a world class athlete, she traveled to America, a country where she knew no one. The author takes the reader on a bumpy, soul searching, heartwarming and sometimes heart-breaking ride. It is a compelling story told with openness, warmth, humor and insight.

www.ingramcontent.com/pod-product-compliance
Lightning Source LLC
Chambersburg PA
CBHW070136080526
44586CB00015B/1720